Taking the Initiative

Patrick Korenblit

KOGAN PAGE

■NETWORK

Kogan Page is the UK member of the Euro Business Publishing Network.
The European members are:
Les Editions d'Organisation, France; Verlag Moderne Industrie, Germany;
Liber, Sweden; Franco Angeli, Italy; and Deusto, Spain.
The Network has been established in response to the growing demand for
international business information and to make the work of Network authors
available in other European languages.

Les Editions d'Organisation, 1992
Translated by Ann Leonard
Illustrated by M Arapu

First published in France in 1993 by
Les Editions d'Organisation, 1 Rue Thénard, 75240 Paris, Cédex 05, France
entitled Vous et .... La Prise d'Initiatives ISBN 2 7081 1530 8

This edition first published in Great Britain in 1994 by
Kogan Page Ltd, 120 Pentonville Road, London Nl 9JN.

British Library Cataloguing in Publication Data.
A CIP record for this book is available from the British Library.

ISBN 0 7494 1195 3

DTP for Kogan Page by
Jeff Carter 197 South Croxted Road, London SE21 8AY

Printed in Great Britain by
Biddles Ltd, Guildford and Kings Lynn

TABLE OF CONTENTS

Introduction *5*
Review your capacity for
  taking initiatives   7

Section 1. *What Is Initiative?* *9*
Give your definition   11   Just beyond the beginning   15
Describe the value of initiative 13   Classifying expressions and proverbs 17

Section 2. *What Are the Company's Needs Concerning Initiative?* *19*
Initiative taking at different levels   How initiatives are expressed   23
  and in different sectors   21

Section 3. *What Questions Arise from Taking the Initiative?* *27*
Diagnose the sources of your
  own initiatives   31

Section 4. *A Few Thoughts on Initiative* *35*
Exercise in timing   37   What reactions do you expect to
Which type are you?   your own initiatives?   45
  Whitman, Wilkes or Woods?   41   Qualifying the stereotypes   47

Section 5. *Styles of Initiatives* *49*
Examine your style of initiative 53   Taking initiatives   54

Section 6. *Taking Initiatives – What Are the Barriers?* *55*
Trace the barriers to your initiatives 61   What happens in your company
                                              to kill off initiative?   63

Section 7. *What Are the Techniques for Taking Initiatives?* **65**
Evaluate your sense of morality and
   your efficiency in taking initiatives 71

Section 8. *Techniques Encouraging People to Take Initiatives* **73**
Assess your ability for encouraging   Do you put educational approaches
   people to take initiatives   77   into actions?   83
What initiative-inciting situations   The tale of the little pony who learns
   do you use?   79   courage   85
Who shall we get to take the
   initiative?   81

Section 9. *Educating Employees to Take Initiatives* **87**
Case study (part 1)   89   Case study (part 2)   91

Final Point. *Evaluate What You Know* **93**
Review your capacity for taking   Also available in the
   initiatives   95   Self-Management Series   96
Ideas about initiative   96

The following symbols are used throughout this book to indicate:

Fill it in.

Find your way.

INTRODUCTION

SCENES FROM COMPANY LIFE

'...You know perfectly well you should have seen to that!

– Not at all, it doesn't come under my responsibility nor is it stipulated in my contract. I think I'm correct in saying that it's So and So's job.

– But you're well aware of the fact that So and So was off on leave that week.

– He ought to have made arrangements to cover for himself and you too. It's not my fault if this department is badly organized, it's your department, I shouldn't have to put up with the consequences!

– Let me tell you something about consequences. Thanks to your thoughtlessness we're going to lose the contract and soon be joining the queues at the dole office!

– If everybody knew who's supposed to do what around here, maybe we could manage to get things done in time.

– We can't foresee everything, you should have taken the initiative in this matter or at least spoken to me about it, if you knew we weren't going to meet the deadline!

– As far as I'm concerned the ball was in your court once I handed the file over to you. And don't talk to me about initiatives, the last one I took really backfired on me, a right telling off and no end of year bonus, so you can keep your initiatives, thanks all the same. Once everybody's clear about departmental objectives then maybe something can be done but in the meantime, as long as we don't know where we stand, it's more a case of personal strategy than initiative!

– So if I don't tell you what you should do, you do nothing? Talk about team work...'

This choice excerpt, taken from a number of conversations between a supervisor and her associate, regardless of the position held by either, must be familiar to you if you have worked in a company of any size or any sector of activity.

It constitutes the starting point of the problem we want to examine:

How do we break the vicious circle which traps both supervisor and employee alike in the web of an inflexible system or puts them at the risk of an ill-considered initiative?

Within the unstable and complex straitjacket which makes up the modern company, each one of us tries to seek out the values which will ensure durability and meet with the support of the majority. Taking initiatives is one value which greatly encourages these virtues.

Yet, in past educational systems and in many existing ones, initiative is excluded, relegated to the ranks of disobedience, often considered to have overtones of rebellion, revolution or the unlawful seizure of power. How did we arrive at this?

Company foundations have been established on the basis of a hierarchical structure and power obtained as much through seniority as through cunning and more recently through knowledge and technical compe-tence. It is because of this that we have come to give initiative the role of the enemy, the undesirable.

The aim of this guide is to give initiative back its stripes, to rehabilitate it and to highlight its virtues and human validity, while remaining conscious of its perverse shifting and limitations. Some of us will find this encounter old-hat, obsolete and unnecessary. Nowadays everyone is convinced of the need to take initiatives, as much for personal as collective development.

While everyone is ready to accept the value of initiative taking, it is interesting to look at a few companies chosen at random, and to gain awareness of the manner in which this conviction is applied in reality.

Rarely has a concept met with such overwhelming general approval and come up against such behavioural resistance.

The company is the mainspring of progress, so it is mainly at the heart of the company that we will study and evaluate the taking of initiatives before proposing a technical and practical approach in response to 2 major questions:

How to take the initiative? And how to encourage initiative taking?

The outline of this guide moves from a discovery of the concept of initiative,

REVIEW YOUR CAPACITY FOR TAKING INITIATIVES

For each statement place a tick on the rising scale from 0 to 100, 0 signifying total disagreement with the statement and 100 registering complete agreement. All positions in between correspond to a level of agreement with the statement.

	0	20	40	60	80	100

1. I willingly take the initiative
2. I prefer to ask others than be asked by them
3. When I take the initiative, I feel like I'm taking a risk
4. I make sure that others perceive or know about my initiatives
5. My initiatives generally meet with approval from others
6. When I come across what I deem to be a good initiative on the part of a fellow team worker or colleague, I congratulate them
7. When I come across what I deem to be a poor initiative on the part of a fellow team worker or colleague, condemning it is not the correct response
8. I would like my fellow team workers to take more initiatives
9. I want to be able to take more initiatives
10. The system, organization or my boss prevent me taking more initiatives
11. Initiative implies results
12. Initiative is an action
13. A company needs initiative at all levels
14. The clearer the objectives the easier it is to take the initiative
15. The role of initiative is to provoke a change of direction
16. Taking the initiative is something that has to be learned
17. Competence is a secondary factor in taking the initiative
18. Lack of recognition is what kills initiative

Interpretation of this evaluation will be revealed through the course of the book. Each item will find its answer in the following chapters. Form your own opinion, we suggest a rendez-vous in the final chapter for taking stock.

where we seek to explain what initiative is, to its application; the main objective is to understand the process of taking initiatives.

....

THE INITIATIVE TO READ THIS BOOK

....

You have already taken the initiative by buying this book, or at least opening it, and whether it was out of curiosity, interest or dire necessity, in my capacity as author, I can only congratulate both of us.

My reaction as instructor, however, is to urge you to determine where you stand regarding this notion of initiative. In other words to analyze:
– how you perceive it
– your understanding of it
– how you apply it.
The survey on page 7 will help you to do this.
Analyzing your responses is a personal affair and only concerns you. You will be the assessed and the assessor. Be relaxed but exact in your responses, this will assist you as you progress through the book.

Section 1
WHAT IS INITIATIVE?

Seeking to define initiative requires research into the meaning of the word, but as in the case of other ideas or notions, its conceptual reality differs from its daily application.

The notion of initiative is essentially a concrete one and it is unnecessary to go into theoretical explanations here. We are interested in the *practical significance* of initiative taking in business and in our daily lives.

In order to understand the term, and successfully develop its application, it is necessary to answer three fundamental questions:

– What is it?
– What is it for?
– How does it work?

These simple questions often help us to obtain immediate operational responses.

WHAT IS IT?

For me, at the outset an initiative is: An act effected for the first time... An action at the beginning of a development... An action which modifies the sequence of events or situations.

The dictionary confirms to some extent this rough outline of a definition of initiative:

1. The ability to initiate things; enterprise... a step... but it goes even further by adding a connotation drawn from the legal world... the power or right to begin something.

It goes on to define a further dimension 'on one's own initiative' as:

2. Quality of one who can act... 'without being prompted by others'.

This twofold dictionary definition underlines the dual quality of this notion of initiative and justifies both our interest in initiative and our preoccupation with trying to understand it.

9

Some of us believe that initiative has been taken once the decision is made and that everything else falls into place. Others prefer to see the outcome of the action before deciding whether or not initiative was involved.

This enlightens us to the fact that each of us judges the taking of initiative differently. In the eyes of one person, so and so is taking the initiative, while in the eyes of another, he is only waiting for his proposal to be implemented.

Initiative taking is more than a theoretical definition; it is the understanding of words and action on them. In other words, it is the action which follows through and applies, in practical terms, the decision taken.

WHAT IS IT FOR?

Some organizational systems preclude all initiative. It can often end up being the grain of sand which clogs the mechanism.

It is difficult to imagine a grain of sand in an hourglass suddenly deciding to stop descending on some pretext (eg that it is warmer above, or that he must attend to an emergency...), or even inciting fellow grains of sand to join him in his act of subversion. The grain of sand, just like a colleague, falls and continues falling according to the law of gravity and just like all the other grains of sand. It 'goes with the flow'.

In another less mechanized, but well run system, like, for example, the army which is characterized by rigorous discipline, initiative may be considered dangerous and, as in this example, punishable by court martial. So we can state that both mechanized systems and human beings are susceptible to rejecting initiative. Hourglasses have been in existence for centuries and armies even longer. This being the case, is it really necessary to worry about initiative? I asked a retired military commander about the importance of initiative. His response was 'Initiative is dangerous!' He then went on to provide me with ample proof that his soldiers' actions during the war were steeped in initiative and that this, among other things, helped them to stay alive.

Our response to the question 'What is initiative for?' depends on our individual position and personal ambition. On the opposite page take the opportunity to express your thoughts on this and establish how important it is for you.

GIVE YOUR DEFINITION

If you still feel the need to consult the dictionary, a first move might be to ask yourself what you automatically assume when you hear the term initiative in everyday common usage.

Try this exercise.

Before turning the page, write below what, in your opinion, initiative really is. You could also note what it is not. This can sometimes be helpful in bringing us closer to the meaning.

For example, we can all agree that initiative serves:
– to get us out of a closed situation;
– to modify the sequence of events;
– to take a committed stance;
– as an extra asset.

HOW DOES IT WORK?

Taking the initiative touches on two different, even opposing, types of practice:
– working by reaction: initiative arises to oppose an unacceptable move already underway;
– working through desire: initiative simply expresses a desire, wish or interest.
Initiative which may be defined as reactionary is the most common form. This is because it is self-justifying. Taking an initiative is breaching something or rebelling in order to justify our act. It is necessary to have sound motives on which to base our self-confidence.
With this type of initiative you will find rebellion or initiative taking as a reaction to an unacceptable or a malevolent act. It is also a moral and human reaction to a perceived danger or wrong.

To sum up, reactive initiative is: 'I must, therefore I do'.
In contrast to this type of initiative we encounter initiative through desire. This is 'I want to, therefore I do'. You could qualify this as 'pro-active'.
Arising from a personal desire unconnected with a context or outside stimulus, this type of initiative is at once the simplest and most difficult to explain.
Simplest because nothing is more direct than desire expressed with no beating about the bush, lending it a force and assurance even though it has perhaps not necessarily been thought through. More complex also because nowadays this spontaneity of desire is tainted with the burden of conscience and inhibition.

ROOTS AND ORIGINS

Initiative has its roots in the Latin verb 'initiare' which means 'to begin'. This gives us a number of words in English with a similar meaning such as: initiate – initial – an initial.
However, it is more than the sense of *beginning* that is present in the word's meaning, but most significantly the notion of *action* which characterizes initiative.

DESCRIBE THE VALUE OF INITIATIVE

Consider your personal as well as your professional situation. Take a few moments to think about and reply to the following questions. Don't look for the right or wrong answer, your opinion is what is important. The rest of this book will reassure you and help you to pinpoint exactly where you stand, but for the present you need a starting point.

What interests have been served by your initiatives?

Whose interests have been served by your initiatives?

In what way have the initiatives of others helped you?

What initiatives have helped you the most?

Why do some initiatives not pay off?

To sum up, in your opinion, what are initiatives for?

The dictionary moreover, defines the term initiative as 'enterprise' which suggests action and progress.

As with good logic everything begins at the beginning. But leading from there are two paths, which can prove to be a source of confusion:

– the path of intention which involves an ill-defined desire, and which in the best possible circumstances, is committed to implementation at the outset but is stalled later on by a lack of conviction. In other cases, it remains indefinitely at this transitional and generally frustrating stage with no progress or achievement to report;

– the other path is that of action which involves desire and the will to succeed and which goes all the way towards finishing the project.

Actually starting a process in itself constitutes action, that of 'opening up', which is, of course, not the same as realizing or achieving that process.

WHAT DO PROVERBS TELL US? AND WHICH ARE YOUR FAVOURITES?

Proverbs are often contradicted by other proverbs, but this balance, which renders it possible to supply a formula to fit just about any situation, is not always used to its fullest advantage.

Some of us are more likely to use 'pro-initiative' proverbs, in other words those which urge us to take initiatives, while others will pepper their conversations and actions with 'anti-initiative' sayings. This indicates a reluctant attitude towards the taking of initiatives.

Try to list those, if any, that you use yourself and draw the necessary conclusions.

The proverbs and sayings that you use:

Anti-initiative	Proverbs	Pro-initiative

JUST BEYOND THE BEGINNING

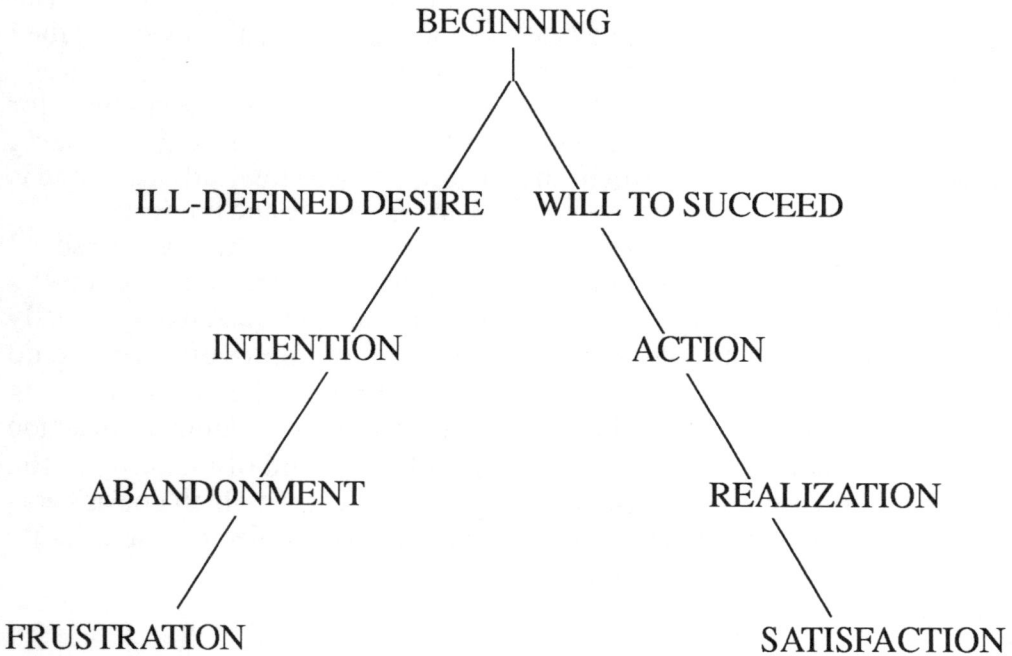

BEGINNING

ILL-DEFINED DESIRE   WILL TO SUCCEED

INTENTION   ACTION

ABANDONMENT   REALIZATION

FRUSTRATION   SATISFACTION

The two paths available to you from the beginning.

• •

HOW PROVERBS INFLUENCE ACTION

• •

Pro-initiative proverbs incite us to act whereas anti-initiative proverbs favour the intention or words as opposed to action and are signs of reserve, or even encouragement to avoid initiatives.

Let's take the two proverbs heading the list: When In Doubt, Don't and Nothing Ventured Nothing Gained.

The first tip advises us not to move, to wait, in order to avoid any possible error. Inertia seems to be the proposed solution.

On the other hand, the second proposes action even in the face of risk. Action seems to be the remedy to every situation.

These proverbs then are neither the whole truth nor totally untrue but may simply be adapted to fit different circumstances, used like the colours on an artist's palette, as they are needed.

They can also be used as a source for reflection: 'When in doubt, ...' think, learn, or try. Here is advice which is both reasonable and prudent.

The proverb, 'Nothing ventured,...' may not be appropriate when the risks are too great and it may actually be wiser and more effective to do nothing rather than do something just for the sake of doing it. An action which is devoid of meaning in the given context, or which doesn't correspond to the objectives set, should be avoided.

CLASSIFYING EXPRESSIONS AND PROVERBS

Here is a list of popular English proverbs which have influenced countless generations. The exercise is to classify them with regard to the cultural and psychological impact they have regarding initiative. If they seem to you to encourage initiative, place a tick in the right hand column (Pro-initiative) and in the left hand column (Anti-initiative) if they appear to discourage it.

Anti-initiative	Proverbs	Pro-initiative
	When in doubt don't	
	Nothing ventured nothing gained	
	Everything comes to those who wait	
	Where there's a will there's a way	
	You can't make an omelette without breaking eggs	
	Once the first step is taken there's no going back	
	As ye sow so shall ye reap	
	Practice makes perfect	
	The leopard doesn't change its spots	
	You've made your bed now you must lie in it	
	No news is good news	
	The road to hell is paved with good intentions	
	Empty vessels make the most noise	
	Always think twice before opening your mouth	
	Strike while the iron is hot	
	It's the thought that counts	
	Well begun is half done	
	Necessity is the mother of invention	
	He who hesitates is lost	
	In for a penny, in for a pound	
	Look before you leap	
	Out of the frying pan into the fire	

Section 2
WHAT ARE THE COMPANY'S NEEDS CONCERNING INITIATIVE?

Companies need initiative in many different ways. The individual enterprise by its very nature needs initiative and it is difficult to conceive of a company or firm surviving very long without it.

Can we talk about a 'market' for initiative? Just as the Stock Exchange is the market for transferrable securities, it is interesting to observe the initiative market, in other words, the confrontation between supply and demand.

The demand for initiative can issue from a recorded decline in performance, for instance, or a customer request, from a supplier or other interested party.

The supply of initiative can be seen at many levels within the company. Initiatives can be taken both by directors and shop floor workers depending on the varying circumstances.

The managing director of a company would be more willing to take initiatives than members of staff, whether because it is the director that has to report back to the shareholders, or more commonly because the managing director wishes to stimulate the company and see it prosper.

In any case, whether through professional conscience or desire to develop or act, the executive, supervisor or shop floor worker can display a capacity for initiative and take action at the heart of the real working operation which will reap results.

Not that these initiatives should short-circuit the hierarchical order, but while still respecting it, they should trigger actions at all levels.

One of the problems that a company may be confronted with in these circumstances is an uncontrolled spate of initiatives which can lead to a power struggle.

The needs expressed by companies in matters of initiative come from various sources.

Creativity, research and competition rapidly spring to mind, but there are

19

several other areas where we can make use of the capacity for initiative.

AREAS WHERE INITIATIVE TAKING IS VITAL

1. Creativity

A company is a prime consumer in constant need of ideas and creativity. The demands of the market, the out-bidding tactics of competitors, the need to maintain your market share and increase it wherever possible make creativity indispensable.

If it is possible to stimulate creativity by constantly adapting methods, the daily required dosage of ideas can only be achieved if each person is encouraged to use their initiative.

2. Availability

A company must make its presence felt on the market in order to survive. Being available to clients, either physically or through relay systems (using all outlets available) is of primary importance and, here again, the driving force behind this availability is initiative.

Fixing a number of appointments may be *adequate* for a sales representative to follow up on his client, but if the idea is to nurture the client, to advise or guide them (which is normal practice for any good sales-person these days), it is not enough. The sales representative must manage these appointments by taking the initiative as to the 'when' (arranging the next meeting), the 'who' (ascertaining the correct targets, the right people to talk to), the 'where' (within the company or outside it) and the 'how' (the contact approach), all of which implies that the salesperson knows the 'why' (the objectives and strategy of the company he represents).

3. Up against 'who does what'

Most companies today are seeking, quite rightly, to better define their activities, fields of operation and parameters. For this, companies separate their structures and personnel in definitions of function. This procedure clearly marks out objectives and job functions but can, in some cases, lead to a certain inflexibility and a real risk of impediment.

Consciousness of the limitations of a function may be beneficial, but it can also become a hindrance.

This is the case in a situation where the work piles up and we take refuge in these limits to avoid doing more than anticipated.

INITIATIVE TAKING AT DIFFERENT LEVELS AND IN DIFFERENT SECTORS

What do you think are the main needs for initiative taking within the ranks of a company?

BY LEVEL
Management ....

....

Chief Executive ....

....

Executive ....

....

Supervisor ....

....

Worker - Employee ....

....

BY SECTOR

Sales	Production	Services

Faced with questions of the 'who does what' type which clarify roles and objectives, we must re-examine the 'man = machine' system and introduce approaches to develop initiative.

4. Research and Development

A good initiative can get us out of a stagnant phase or risky situation and solve a pressing problem. Such an action is appreciated for the immediate benefits it affords, but the wider implications are even more beneficial. A generally improved attitude towards initiative taking within the company enables us to face the future with resolution and determination.

A Research and Development Service is a structure which both demands and taps initiative.

The development of a company does not follow a regular pattern. It isn't a river that knows no turning, but a sequence of making headway and retreating, and of standing still. These movements are engendered by the sometimes unconnected initiatives taken by the participants (searchers or users).

Each initiative, bearing in mind the margin for manoeuvre in such a service, gives rise to a budget on which the company expects a return but knows that only a small part will actu-ally lead to something productive. Initiative, in this case, is costly but every company knows that lack of initiative can be a great deal more costly.

5. Quality

Another demand on initiative taking is the search for quality. Whether in the context of short- or long-term action, the need to see employees taking shifts in reflection, responsibility and innovation, continually calls for individual initiative or collective proposals.

From now on, it is no longer conceivable or acceptable that an employee be seen merely as a hired hand for the company. New economic and social imperatives demand that we need employees who constantly and actively 'think'.

Striving for quality demands that human resources should be of good quality, and that every employee share a commitment to the company and the product or service.

6. Competition

In a free open market, a company is, by definition, in competition. Being the first to attempt and succeed at something new is the deciding factor. Competition is the stimulus for initiatives for all companies.

✎ HOW INITIATIVES ARE EXPRESSED

Do you think there exists a lack of initiative taking in your company or do you think that the initiatives taken adequately cover company needs? How is the need for initiative expressed in your company? The chart below aims to help you discover the sources of demand for initiative within your organization.

	Sector needing initiatives	Who	Example of a need for initiative taking	Results
CREATIVITY				
AVAILABILITY				
UP AGAINST 'WHO DOES WHAT'				
DEVELOPMENT				
QUALITY				
COMPETITION				
COMMITMENT				
CONFRONTATION				
CHANGE				
HUMAN POTENTIAL				

An important stimulus to initiative is the desire to be first or the leader in your field. The competitive spirit, the challenging of others stimulates individual initiative.

The effect of competition on initiative is like that of heat on water: it brings it to the boil.

7. Commitment

What criteria does a teacher use to evaluate and recognize his students, a boss his employees, or a company its personnel?

Results, of course, are essential to the evaluation of a student or employee. Good teachers, however, evaluate performance on the basis of potential and effort as much as results. Some companies only look at results but increasingly others are taking into account the manner and level of personal commitment of each member of staff. Commitment emerges as a major criterion in evaluating individuals within a company.

Initiative directly expresses the degree of this commitment. But not just any initiative. It is not a rare thing to come across a situation where trade union opposition is sufficient reason to cancel any form of reward or recognition for the employee concerned. This lack of recognition felt by the employee could be the reason for his trade union involvement in the first place but that is another matter. Trade union membership is one way of taking the initiative, but it may be perceived by the employer as tending away from commitment to the company.

In an inverse situation, a boss may appeal to employees to stand for election as staff representatives, in a bid to improve employer–staff relations and in these circumstances, initiative has changed camp.

Initiative is a better yardstick for measuring an employee's potential and motivation than any form of obedience. It is through examining initiative taking that a company can see the real value of an employee's contribution.

8. Progress through confrontation and conflict

One of the driving forces of progress is the confrontation of ideas. Any company that tries to eliminate its conflicts and tensions by ignoring them, will find itself experiencing a period of stagnation or even regression and no headway will be possible. So, how does confrontation manifest itself? Confrontation occurs as a result of different or even divergent positions emerging in any given situation. The conflict arising may be between employees, between employers and staff or between different departments making different but simultaneous demands on one resource, eg accounts and sales may have conflicting needs when choosing the company computer system. In every case, a situation arises where re-assessment and re-evaluation are needed, and initiatives taken to resolve the problem.

The more the confrontation demands a confirmed and concrete position, the more it requires initiative. The risk-taking involved here as well as the hypothetical value, make initiative a fundamental component of the confrontation or conflict as a generator of progress.

9. Change

Some changes come about of themselves but often change is deliberately undergone. Preparation for change is the best guarantee of success.

This preparation is characterized by initiative which always tries to gain the upper hand on fate.

Changes are a frequent feature of company life and they will increase. Attitudes of undergoing or tolerating changes must give way to one of facing up to them in the first instance and taking control of them afterwards. Understanding the impending changes does not necessarily imply control of them and opposition may arise.

Change, however, needs to test the waters, to try out new methods and discover strategies. Initiative constitutes the dynamic force which will trigger change but also and most importantly, see it through.

10. Highlighting human potential (beyond skills)

Human Resource management taps into and acknowledges the value of initiative. But beware! Avoid counting on skills alone. Instead, aim to take into account and develop human qualities in an individual and in particular in management, which are often lacking where they are needed most.

Often initiative is identified rapidly, doubtless due to its scarcity, and one of two things will happen. Either it is suppressed as the system won't tolerate it, or it is very quickly appreciated.

In the first case, the individual who has taken the initiative will know what's going on and take himself elsewhere in search of recognition. This initiative will be an easy one for him or her to take.

In the second case, this recognition can sometimes direct him or her along surprising career paths, irregular in their scheme of leaps and omissions, rather like the pattern of a gifted child skipping classes where others struggle and falter.

Initiative in this case can manage to delude others who lack the necessary courage and have only temerity or recklessness. The admiration aroused in those who lack initiative makes them blind. It is particularly important, then, to make the distinction between a one-off initiative, even if it is very spectacular, and a really consistent spirit of initiative which is essential for a head of Human Resources, or even at top management level in any company.

Section 3
WHAT QUESTIONS ARISE FROM TAKING THE INITIATIVE?

Initiative appears in many forms and gives rise to various questions which a company should not underestimate. To understand the extent of what lies behind this we need to examine how the problem of initiative arises in a variety of contexts. We then need to ask what questions it raises for both you and your company.

SITUATIONS AND PEOPLE

Situations where initiative plays a role are often linked with relationships between individuals. Let us examine this in the following cases:

Initiative and the child

A child's education is aimed at socialization. It concerns making a child understand that the best form of behaviour is that which is socially acceptable.

Learning good manners, politeness and the norms of society, triggers a further system of dependence in the child, as he leaves his natural dependence behind.

His capacity for initiative however, remains linked to a child's spontaneity and the wish to satisfy his desires. For some, social conventions remain secondary and less important than their own gratification. They are hungry to satisfy their desires. For others, this educative yoke creates an undeniable limitation to their movements and initiatives.

The role of modern teaching in relation to the child is to open up the paths of initiative by counterbalancing the weight of norms, rules and other limitations or prohibitions, with stimuli, thus encouraging a greater level of participation and involvement.

A child's development requires an increase in autonomy, and initiative is a sign of autonomy. But don't forget that in order to pass from the dependency phase to the autonomous phase we come up against conflicting phases of counter-dependence and dependence.

The problem a child experiences in his dealings with others and in particular with his peers is expressed in:
– Who started it?
– It wasn't me, it was him!
– No it's not my fault, it's his!
Unless it's
– It's thanks to me...

BEHIND THE CHILD'S DIRECT SPEECH IS THE IDEA OF COMPETITION. THIS EMERGES AS A FORCE BEHIND INITIATIVE AND PUNISHMENT MAY THEN CHECK OR EVEN INHIBIT INITIATIVE.

Initiative and the philosopher

Each philosophy, culture or belief provides a framework for initiative through commandments, precepts or lines of conduct.

The Fatalist will not share the same vision or action as the political activist. But beyond dogma, philosophy provides us with part of the answer.

The philosopher wonders about the freedom of thought and action, visualizing the connection between thought and action or politics. This reasoning once again, should be logical enough to be workable.

Philosophy works to make choice possible for the individual. As long as choice does not exist, a capacity for initiative cannot be evaluated but once it does exist, initiative becomes a character trait.

A prisoner has no need to ask himself where he will go as he must remain where he is. As soon as he is released this question arises and for many the deprivation of initiative will have diminished their capacity for action. But for others this new found freedom allows them to actively express everything they couldn't during their incarceration.

Choice is thus essential for the philosopher unless he is an existentialist thinker, who like Sartre, considers himself 'condemned to be free'. This only serves to reinforce the intensity of the issue.

> THE QUESTION WHICH THE PHILOSOPHER RAISES WITH REGARD TO INITIATIVE IS THAT OF CHOICE.

Politics and the military

In an international conflict like the Gulf War, for instance, initiative seemed unacceptable if not detestable.

During the period which followed the invasion of Kuwait up until the intervention by American armed forces, the war relied on dissuasion tactics (embargo, threats, etc) and appeals (freeing of hostages, peace plan proposals, etc). But each subsequent stage in the escalation of the war on both sides had to be presented by each as a response to hostile enemy initiative. Everything resembling an initiative was laid at the feet of the opposing camp, thus holding them responsible for the conflict. Each camp assumed the role of victim and therefore had the right to defend itself. This legitimate defence relieved them of the guilt of being the attackers, especially in the eyes of public opinion.

This was the role of the political side of things relayed by the media. The military role was to take tactical and strategic initiatives without lending arguments to the enemy, thus apparently leaving the field open for the politicians.

On the western side, the effect consisted of taking initiatives, but disguising or minimizing them in the face of opinion in order to avoid blame which brings about trouble and loss of confidence. For Iraq it was the right, even the obligation imposed by the 'Holy War', in other words divine will, which exempted them from any blame arising from their initiatives.

> THIS ILLUSTRATES A MAJOR PROBLEM: TAKING INITIATIVES CAN ENGENDER BLAME AND IT IS IMPORTANT TO KNOW HOW TO ESCAPE IT.

Man and woman

Between a couple, the relationship is modified according to events, but it is certain that both parties influence the development of the relationship.

We all know couples who seem to have one-sided relationships; in other words, it always seems to be the same party who takes the initiative rather than the other. Two possibilities present themselves: either we don't have access to the hidden side of this couple's life, or this imbalance will end up putting pressure on the relationship, and could lead to a breakup. A relationship between a couple can only last if there is give and take, if it is a relationship involving interchange and alternation of initiatives. In any case, as with war, every movement, every word and gesture, is perceived and interpreted in such a way as to appear like an initiative.

In general, convention presents the man as predominantly being the one to take the initiative, but as the saying goes, 'man proposes, woman disposes', which suggests that, in fact, *she* is the one to take the initiative.

Keep in mind that not everyone has the same capacity for initiative and also that relationships conceal imbalances. However, we must remain conscious of the fact that where there is deadlock and inaction, there is little hope for the couple to continue to develop a relationship.

A characteristic example of this situation is established by the frequent breakdown of a relationship when one party decides to follow a course of psychoanalytic treatment. The relationship is altered, expectations are different…, the balance is upset.

THE QUESTION RAISED CONCERNING INITIATIVE BETWEEN THE COUPLE IS THAT OF RECIPROCITY WHICH CAN BE INTERPRETED AS THE BALANCE OF GIVE AND TAKE. INITIATIVE CAN THUS APPEAR AS A MARK OR MEASURE OF AFFECTION, OR LOVE OF OR FOR ONE ANOTHER.

Initiative and the psychoanalyst
With the insight of psychoanalysis, taking initiatives adopts a new dimension.

In the case of the child it is a matter of learning to end dependency and to manipulate the occasionally inhibitive pressure of the superego. In simple terms to stop obeying blindly.

Elsewhere we saw that it involved the important issue of erasing the guilt which blocks initiative. But to arrive at 'how to resolve difficulties' the psychoanalyst recommends that we discover the sources of the block. It's not always enough to talk about them but in many cases it will help.

What makes initiative taking difficult is that it implies the capacity to manage guilt-inducing situations, to deal with them fully and accept responsibility for an act undertaken in good faith.

DIAGNOSE THE SOURCES OF YOUR OWN INITIATIVES

How does the problem of initiative present itself for you? Analyze a recent situation or change which has taken place in your home or workplace.

What was the origin of this change? Who was responsible for the initiative for this change?

What are the dominant issues characterizing your dread of initiative?
On the 6 axis, determine the foundations of your initiatives.
Mark from 0 - 5 in order to obtain your initiative polygon.

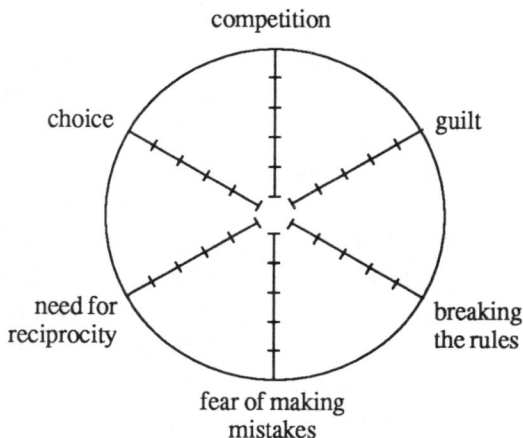

competition

choice

guilt

need for
reciprocity

breaking
the rules

fear of making
mistakes

Use this polygon to evaluate whether it corresponds to what you wished for, both in terms of the image you want to give and the reality of what you want to do.
It could also be used to obtain feedback from a person whose judgement is important to you. Your immediate superior for example.

It is an opportunity to break rules and avoid compliance which links us to the Oedipal resolution, ie, that of ending dependency.

So, initiative should not be confused with going into action which is unconscious or childlike, but on the contrary should be considered as conscious decision and action intended to modify a situation.

FOR THE PSYCHOANALYST, THE OEDIPAL DIMENSION OF INITIATIVE, MEANING THE ENDING OF DEPENDENCY AND BREAKING RULES, CONSTITUTES THE MAJOR QUESTION.

The executive and the employee

A company is a privileged and fertile environment for taking initiatives, as much through external promptings as through its own projects, and provides a context for relationships and communication generally favourable to taking initiative.

However, this environment, as we have seen in the introduction, doesn't always produce the desired response in this area.

What, in real terms, is the problem and why does this huge deficiency exist?

In the first place, we lay the blame for one of the major causes of lack of initiative on the companies themselves.

The popular and firmly anchored archetypes at the heart of institutions like the church and the army, do not promote an example which embraces initiative. It is often considered as contrary to the rules and deserving of severe punishment.

Let's consider the case of A and one of his employees B.

What expectations can A have regarding B?

A wants to feel secure in his trust in B, meaning that B does what has been agreed, but furthermore that he will procure or ask for the means to overcome any eventual obstacles which crop up as quickly as possible.

A also expects that above and beyond what was agreed, B will intervene when something doesn't seem to be functioning properly.

Finally, and perhaps most importantly, A wants B to keep him informed of what has been done by giving him an efficient summary of the situation as it progresses.

For his part, B has, depending on his temperament and in his capacity as A's assistant, multiple expectations regarding his boss.

First of all he wants to have the confidence of A. This means that B has an implied or clearly defined zone where he has freedom of action and can take initiatives within a defined range. This means that there is a degree of personal contribution at the centre of the carrying out and even the planning stages of his work. In return for this contribution B expects some form of recognition from A. This will fuel his resolve and permit him to continue.

In principle, these expectations should be compatible and meet with mutual satisfaction. However, functioning along the lines of trust involves a high risk factor. The risks of going wrong are multiple, frequent and rarely controllable.

Also, trust should not be blindly consenting but constructed step by step.

A whole series of various factors can have the effect of diminishing trust in the other party:

– rumours
– not endorsing an action
– not recognizing an action
– contradiction between word and deed
– misinterpretation of an intention
– keeping back information
– lack of sincerity in exchanges
– short circuits in relations
– spontaneous suspicion
– possibility of jealousy.

Faced with all these risks, every decision, every act is an opportunity to challenge this trust and consequently the dynamics reverse and the process is blocked until it descends into distrust.

This phenomenon rapidly terminates the room for initiative supplied by A. He no longer tolerates it outside of B's defined action zone, even to the point of reducing that zone.

As for B, depending on his temperament, either he stops taking the initiative, deciding that he's not paid for it, or he continues to take it but steps further and further out of bounds in order to force A to react or to embarrass him.

> WITHIN THE COMPANY ONE OF THE MAJOR RESISTANCES TO TAKING INITIATIVES REMAINS THE DANGER OF MAKING MISTAKES AND THE FEAR THIS EVOKES. IT IS THROUGH THE CAPACITY OF EXECUTIVES AND EMPLOYEES TO ASSUME RESPONSIBILITY FOR THESE MISTAKES THAT THE DIFFERENCE IN PERFORMANCES WILL MANIFEST ITSELF.

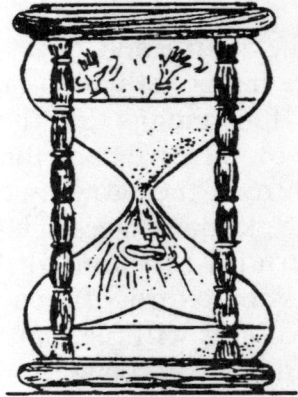

Section 4
A FEW THOUGHTS ON INITIATIVE

DERIVATION

The practised eye of the linguist will linger over the work 'initiative' with interest, not just because of the four 'i's it contains – few words can boast such a profusion of this vowel – but also for its significance in other complex combinations.

'In'

With a more light-hearted glance, we can indulge in playing a game of words rather than an intense etymological study. The first thing we notice about 'initiative' is the 'in' at the beginning. 'In' can be regarded as a prefix signifying interior, something coming from within, which would tie in with our previous presentation of initiative, based on desire or the pro-active. A reactive initiative, however, can be perceived as coming from the exterior or to use an invented word, 'exitative'.

'In' can also be used as a prefix of negation signifying 'un' or 'not' such as in 'insignificant', 'invisible' or 'inedible', suggesting that there should exist an opposite of the word initiative, which as we shall see is not immediately evident.

Worse still, the term 'initiative' does not possess an opposite; as inaction is the opposite of action, which obliges us to label those who don't take the initiative as 'lacking in initiative'.

INITIATIVE AND TIME

One of the dilemmas facing the sales assistant who is trying to make a client sign a contract, is the timing of negotiations. Depending on the service or product being proposed, this timing can vary significantly.

A shop assistant will be confronted with the choice of the moment to launch into a sales pitch or even simply to address the client observing the window display – you have surely noticed that a car salesman is rarely the first to speak, as if his instructions were: 'Wait for them to come to you or you'll make them run away'.

At the other end of the scale, you could expect the sale of nuclear power plants to necessitate several years of negotiation, and that, depending on economic, environmental and political factors, it would be a matter of choosing the right moment for taking the initiative.

When an appointment is made and duly kept between a seller and a buyer, each leaves the other with a series of questions intended to develop negotiations. Except in the case of a subsequent appointment already being fixed, the salesperson tends to wonder when he should next make contact: not too soon, so as not to appear too eager and put himself at a disadvantage vis-a-vis the buyer, not too late, so as not to miss the boat when he could have made his mind up.

Good salespeople know how to establish their relations with clients in order to minimize the risk of this type of uncertainty. But often the doubts exist and so time-management in taking initiatives is an important factor in a company's daily routine.

The signing of a contract – and ultimately the company's turnover figures – depend on the correct evaluation of the time when the initiative should be taken.

EXERCISE IN TIMING

List the areas/situations in your professional environment where you consider the timing of initiative taking is essential.

_____

_____

_____

_____

_____

_____

List the areas/situations in your personal life where the timing of your initiatives is important.

_____

_____

_____

_____

_____

_____

37

INDEPENDENCE AND AUTONOMY

Companies are always on the lookout for new ideas, for creative achievement or the capacity for imagination and action. Initiatives constitute the cornerstones of the structure; each initiative must be practical and workable.

Depending on the context and style of company management, an initiative can seem to be a constructive element – a foundation on which to build – or a destructive instrument apt to undermine the fragile foundations or collide with the more solid ones.

In the same environment one action may be experienced or considered as a positive initiative or a subversion.

What distinguishes these two situations are the structure and adaptability at the heart of the company's ethos and especially the sort of guidelines which govern inter-personal and inter-group relationships.

An action in a context where the objectives are imprecise or unclear or in which the people do not believe will give rise to behaviour which we will call 'deviant'.

Those adept at deviant behaviour look for limits they can't find, put forward claims of lack of long term vision, absence of strategy, and at the same time don't accept any control of their own behaviour. They consider themselves the only parties likely to act competently.

In such a context, an initiative can only be taken as a proof of subversion, everyone working out – probably with some justification – his own objectives, without reference to or coordination with other people, and, without asking for help.

Such employees behave in an independent way.

They do things alone and for themselves since there are no real communal demands: 'I do what I want and nobody can tell me otherwise.' It is through this different context that initiative takes on its real meaning.

Any boss would be only too delighted to discover an employee acting on his own along the lines of in-house policies and objectives.

On the other hand, the initiative of an employee in a vague context, lacking definite orientation, will be perceived by the boss either as the expression of a bad mood or subversion, in any case as independence or even a bid to seize power.

INITIATIVE IN SEXUAL RELATIONS

In order to understand how initiative functions, reference to the sexual domain could help us. Not that relations in a company are similar to those between a couple, but studying this relationship highlights what initiative really is as opposed to intention.

Whether we look at animals or humans we can state that introductions, courting and foreplay are often necessary to the sexual act. The question: 'Who started it?' often goes unanswered.

Is it the woman, by dressing provocatively or simply elegantly? Is it the man by his invitation to dance or have a drink?

We could consider the answer to be: whoever directly addressed the other first. But this isn't an initiative for a relationship and even less so for a sexual one.

There is a whole procedure made up of chance events and choices.

Let's analyze the sexual relationship of a couple with several years of communal living already behind them. From the moment when they find themselves in bed together, what leads to the sexual act?

The desire of one of them is a priority factor. Then the arousal of desire in the other by means of words or more often by touch which will not be directly explicit, but in the form of diversion, sometimes as play, sometimes by consecutive stages with positive regular feedback, will allow them to get down to the act or

at least to the stage where one can be sure the other wants it too.

But the game doesn't end there. The fact of having adhered to the project does not necessarily imply agreement with the method or approach of the partner. He (or she) has needs of his own which may not directly correspond with his partner's.

So it is a matter of finding what is appropriate, the role of each in the scenario of the other and trying to create a situation where the two approaches tolerate one another reasonably well, for communication reaching the heights of communion is only rarely achieved and risks shattering certain illusions, or creating new ones.

Consequently, some will consider it more satisfying to manage a complete coupling, with no holding back, with complete abandon, while maintaining free will and personal fantasy throughout.

REAL OR FAKE INITIATIVES

The expectation of initiative on the part of the employee or company should be considered carefully.

The employee who expresses it may do so in three different ways.

Let's consider Messrs Whitman, Wilkes and Woods, three executives in the same company.

Whitman really does take initiatives and generally talks about their effects more often than the reasons for them. It is the actions which are analyzed but he himself does not consider them to be initiatives. The term initiative is more often used by those around him to define or qualify his actions.

Whitman doesn't feel the same way as often his 'initiative' – he would be more likely to say : his act – seems natural to him, but this is not necessarily the case in the eyes of others, for whom the act in question appears to be reactive to the context or to create an unusual or unexpected move.

Mr Wilkes is a different man. He says he takes initiatives. In fact, it's more often a question of actions or, even more restrictively, decisions going as far as a trial stage but not going much further.

Wilkes displays an inconsistent attitude, is sometimes determined but his initiatives are conventional and only take place in a given setting, at best in conjunction with a move already under way.

The third of our guinea pigs, Mr Woods, is a reactive critic. His ini-

WHICH TYPE ARE YOU?
WHITMAN, WILKES OR WOODS?

Read the description of the different characters. Do you consider yourself closer in attitude to Whitman, Wilkes or Woods?

....

....

Have you ever known or do you know any Whitmans, Wilkes Or Woods?

Whitman ....

....

Wilkes..

....

Woods...

....

How do you deal with the 'initiatives' of each?

....

....

....

....

tiatives are ideas which contest. In some cases it is a matter of rebellion but in general it is his way of opposing an established system.

In effect, his opposition is expressed by claiming that given the context and management dominated style, one cannot take initiatives. He invokes shortcomings as the basis of his challenge and seeks to blame these deficiencies on the established power system as if its sole mission was the authorization of initiatives.

Let's not forget that an initiative is taken and not given in any circumstances nor is it authorized through differences with a power or delegation. Here we hit on the heart of the problem. Initiative is, in psychoanalytic terms, the Oedipus resolution of the executive or employee within the company ranks. It is a truly adult action, accepted by the one who executes it, which signifies that the person is able to justify it before his superiors without feeling embarrassment or guilt.

Initiative can be in opposition to the orientation of a hierarchy but it can also be the object of a new attitude, neither submissive nor opposing, allowing the opening up or development of an innovative path or contribution of a different solution.

How could we imagine that the hierarchy could accept and even condone the taking of initiatives by its employees, in other words to take a direction other than the one indicated? Isn't this a contradiction?

AN INITIATIVE AT ALL TIMES

If initiative is a prompt action which offers a new opening, then a company has a persistent need which makes initiative indispensable at all times, at all levels and in all areas.

In a general way, a company has entered a process which involves dealing with the problem of who does what through a more precise definition of roles and more rigorous and better structured organizational approaches.

These concepts of working can only be of benefit, if not in terms of efficiency, then at least in terms of the company's culture and development. An over-organized system of working can lead to a closed and paranoic system where everything ends up being regulated and nothing left to chance.

Fortunately, such an over formalized world is unrealistic, both from the point of view of the directors' global wishes, even if some of them may feel some inclination towards this plan, and because it is simply unworkable. It is not possible to control absolutely everything. Let's not forget that a major strength of a company – perhaps particularly so for the service industries – is the flexibility that can be shown when a new change of direction takes place, or more simply when procedures are no longer there to say what has to be done.

When this flexibility does not exist, it is the functioning of the process which takes over and which creates blocked structures, which is exactly what administrations are struggling against nowadays. For them the way forward is a long time coming, because of the stultifying effect of established procedures and habits.

So, how do we preserve this flexibility without becoming lax or *laissez-faire*? Here it is wiser and more efficient to tap into a person's individual capacities.

Each little thing requires special attention, and we don't consider the employee who sweeps up around his work post at the end of the day or the executive who takes a moment to tidy his desk before leaving, in the same way as those who need constant repetition of these instructions day after day. In the interests of cleanli-ness in the one case and security in the other, you may have to end up making internal regulations which run the risk of being ignored.

As we feel bound to point out, not everyone spontaneously takes these initiatives and for such people it is necessary to employ other methods. For example, the method of 'you've made your bed so you shall lie on it'. The idea is to try to obtain compliance without bringing pressure to bear, simply by giving the rules of the job and subsequently allowing the individual concerned to find out the consequences for himself. But here again, this doesn't always work. The method of 'nothing ventured nothing gained', is aimed at showing what's at stake, in other words, the comparison between what is to be gained by taking the initiative and what can be lost by not doing so.

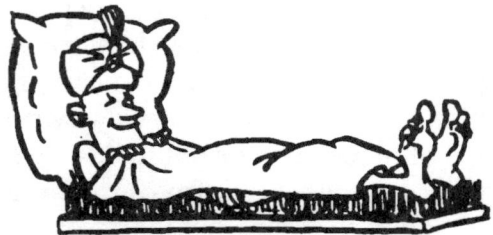

RISK OF INITIATIVE AND OF NON-INITIATIVE

Taking the initiative often implies taking a risk. It intervenes, in effect, into a given context where the initiative will modify, change, upset. It creates a new situation and this change isn't easily achieved.

There is a risk of being wrong, and there are risks too in the necessity of assuming responsibility for choices and actions.

But let's not forget that without these initiative the risks could be even greater. Doing nothing or not taking a decision can have much graver consequences than a misjudged decision or action.

Better to shout 'Fire!' and get out of a burning building fast, even if in a disorderly fashion, than to wait until this option is no longer a possibility.

Better to work on existing product lines as the market evolves than to wait until customers are no longer buying the first product, before planning the next. Of course here we're playing with caricatures, but companies are confronted every day with the choice 'to do or not to do'. So, they can decide in favour of one option of the other, but the choice to do nothing is very often a cop-out, a statement of deficiency which does not really correspond to a decision but on the contrary to a lack of decision. In this case the resistant system perpetuates itself... A lack of initiative can be expensive.

DIFFERENCE BETWEEN A GOOD AND A BAD INITIATIVE

What distinguishes a good initiative from a bad one?

The same decision taken by a person and followed up by decided action can in effect turn out to be a good or a bad thing depending on whether or not it is in line with company policy and objectives.

So the success of an initiative depends to some extent on its intrinsic value but even more on its relation to the context and to 'others'.

By definition an initiative implies an unasked for and unauthorized action, meaning one which requires an advanced degree of autonomy. But if the attitude underlining the initiative arises more from a desire for independence than from autonomy, there is great risk that this initiative triggers off suspicion, mistrust or

WHAT REACTIONS DO YOU EXPECT TO YOUR OWN INITIATIVES?

What are your boss's reactions to your initiatives?

1. Optimism (it's going to work) ❏
2. Pessimism (it won't work because...) ❏
3. Realism (you're given the means to make it work) ❏
4. Prudence (analyze the risks and precautions to be taken) ❏
5. Recklessness (let's go for it!) ❏
6. Insensitivity (there's no point in telling me about it) ❏
7. Criticism (it's not the right procedure,
   you should have spoken to me first) ❏
8. Support (what can I do to help you?) ❏
9. Simplification (it's simple, all you have to do is...) ❏
10. Complication (nothing's as easy as that, have you considered...) ❏

Determine the three attitudes you would like to see from your boss

....

Determine the three attitudes you would not like to see in your boss:

....

Tell him so, it could be useful for both of you.

break-down rather than leading to cohesion and confidence.

An understanding of a company's or institution's objectives, strategies and orientations is necessary to the success of an initiative.

This means that a boss cannot be content to hope that his employees guess his projects, policies or desires. He must inform them so that they can formulate and clarify them. He can then be more assured of their comprehension and cooperation.

A bad initiative can be a sign of a misunderstanding of, or non-adherence to, the objectives set out. It is a signal demanding clarification or quite simply expression: a request to 'set out the objectives'.

All too often the dream turns to a nightmare once we are no longer able to define and say what we expect from the other party. Your employee is on the lookout for clues; advancing on tip-toes, he tries a sign of good will, but on getting no response either positive or negative, his initiatives become assertive or even subversive, giving rise to suppression and the start of a deterioration in relationships.

COUNTRIES, CULTURES AND INITIATIVE

More and more detailed studies are being carried out on a European and international scale, on the subject of company managers and employees.

The internationalization of careers, the creation of European Union and the obligatory exchanges with other cultures make it necessary for us to understand other ways of thinking and acting.

At the risk of crude caricaturization, while seeking to discern the dominant character traits of a culture, it is possible to understand the ways in which company representatives from different cultures take initiatives.

Initiative, as we have seen, is a necessity for each and every company and a source of success. Depending on individual attitudes, the impact and results will be different.

We will find in each culture, in each country and in each company, unusual or marginal individuals, differing from the clichéd image or the preconceived notions we might have about the behaviour of these cultures.

A Frenchman can be tough, committed and have a sense of duty but this doesn't correspond in this case with

QUALIFYING THE STEREOTYPES

The table below gives an image of the ways in which representatives from each culture express themselves at the initiative stage.
Where possible draw on your personal experiences to qualify or correct these 'caricatures'.

Cultures	Way of taking initiative	Origins	Your experience
French	by the individual	desire to do things differently	
German	discipline and organization	thoroughness necessity	
American	pioneer golden boy	naiveté, interest, lack of history	
Japanese	kamikaze harakiri	tradition duty	
Italian	system D	combination, palaver, interest	
Spanish	bullfighter	glory duty	
English	voluntary	desire for independence	
Dutch	trade	commercial interest	
Eastern bloc countries	lacking initiative	system excluding initiative	

Compare wherever possible your experiences of relations with your foreign associates. Do they seem to you more or less likely to take initiatives? In what ways?

what characterizes normal French behaviour. A Japanese person can be flighty, badly brought up or a trickster but again this would be outside the norm or an exceptional case.

Also let's keep in mind that everybody preserves his personality but that dominant and characteristic traits do emerge from a culture, perhaps moreover under the influence of it.

INITIATIVE, ONE WAY OF REDUCING COMPLEXITY

Nowadays companies are faced with complexity and a need to change which can easily run out of control. The multiplicity of elements which enter into strategic or management decisions contribute to this complexity.

Initiative is one way of reducing this complexity. In the past, rules were thought to be enough to determine the dual behaviour of approval or rejection, and were easy to control. Nowadays, the tidal wave of suggestions, propositions and initiatives issuing from all sources and provoking direct and secondary consequences at any level may have to be con-

trolled but they do, no doubt, constitute an asset. At the same time they present a problem of the complication of relations and systems which companies, for the most part, have no idea yet how to cope with.

Anything which aims to simplify is interpreted as manipulative or false. Seeking to simplify what is complex means reduction and must thus be wrong thinking.

Only clarification enables us not to limit the complexity but to understand it and be able to develop with it and even manage it.

Clarifying, not simplifying

The opposition of these two apparently similar terms is significant. In company strategy whereas simplification compels obedience, clarification actually permits understanding. Developing initiative is not realized by creating reflexes of obedience but on the contrary by providing the means to understand.

Section 5
STYLES OF INITIATIVES

It is easy to pinpoint the dominant characteristics of a company employee or executive if we examine their entire spectrum of attitudes and behaviour.

Each person possesses a degree of capacity for initiative in the quantitative sense of the term. But apart from this scale we notice differences in the manner of taking initiatives. These qualitative differences allow us to distinguish styles of initiative.

This dimension is fundamental as the style of an initiative will influence its success. You may take any number of initiatives in the course of a day without one of them leading to a satisfactory conclusion. At the other end of the scale you may only very rarely take an initiative but it systematically turns out to be applicable and fruitful.

The spectrum on which attitudes to initiative are determined is the tendency for action – we could say Pro-Action – to mark the difference from the other extreme point of the spectrum, reaction.

In fact, the style of initiative is first of all linked to the fact that some people take initiatives in reaction to a situation while others have a spontaneous desire to act.

But this spectrum can be split up into an array of colours ranging from blue at one extreme to red at the other passing through shades of purple. We are now going to identify some which correspond to initiative-taking attitudes.

PRO-ACTIVITY
/
DESIRE-WANT
/
CONVICTION
/
PROVOCATION
/
NEED
/
DISPUTE
/
REBELLION-REVOLT
/
REACTIVITY

∙∙∙∙∙∙∙∙∙∙∙∙∙∙∙∙∙∙∙∙∙∙∙∙∙∙∙∙∙∙

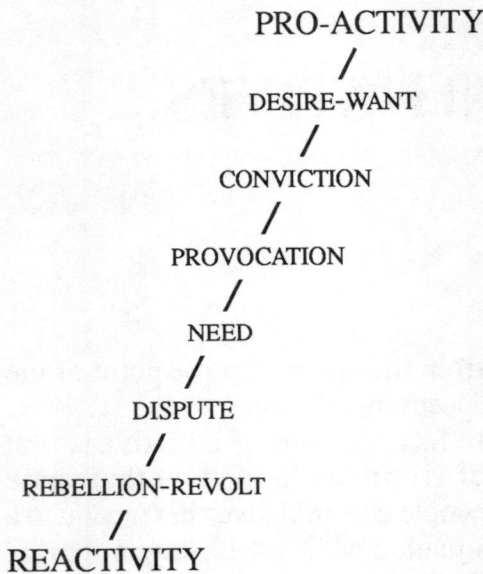

FROM REACTIVITY TO PRO-ACTIVITY

∙∙∙∙∙∙∙∙∙∙∙∙∙∙∙∙∙∙∙∙∙∙∙∙∙∙∙∙∙∙

Reactivity manifests itself in the most explicit way by **REBELLION** or **REVOLT**.

The initiative is taken against a restrictive situation which is becoming unbearable. Consequently, the initiative becomes a valve for expressing disagreement in a violent and direct way in the form of an attempt to take power. The most simple example of this would be a mutiny on board a ship, where the crew decides to reverse the balance of power by taking it by force.

Within a company it is not necessary to resort to force to demonstrate a rebellious attitude. An action opposing decisions already made can be an expression of rebellion and can bring about a reversal of previous trends or relationships and a takeover of power. We encounter such attitudes in situations where roles are unclear, employees have little control over their actions and latent conflicts are not dealt with.

DISPUTE is also a reactive basis on which to take initiatives.

It is not necessarily a question of seizing power but of weakening it. The situation provoking such an initiative is again restrictive. The challeging attitude is expressed by initiatives which remain realistic.

This is typical in the case of trade union initiatives and strikes among others, which while remaining within the bounds of the union and legality and thus the system, demonstrate the disagreement of these organizations in relation to the restrictive situation.

The primary source of reactivity is **NEED**. It is as a result of a need for something, something lacking which is becoming necessary, that initiative will emerge in this case.

Initiative based on an attitude of need is the easiest to justify and is, moreover, the most common form used.

It even happens quite frequently that we make an initiative of the 'reactive' type pass for a 'pro-active' type by attaching to it the justification of need and necessity.

An executive will make his decisions based on his own interests but will justify them by citing his departmental needs.

PROVOCATION is a particular mode of initiative. It is here that we cross over the frontier between the Reactive and the Pro-active.

Provocation may be triggered by any number of different causes. But whatever the cause behind it, we are more interested in its effect, that is to say, the actions which are a result of the provocation. It is even this which help us to define provocation: action or words that *trigger a reaction.*

In a company provocation takes various forms which range from sarcastic comments at decisions taken by others (bosses or colleagues) to rebellious acts which pass through all the intermediary levels to induce a reaction (unjustified delays, files not dealt with...).

However, the most obvious active aspects of provocation are in decline. It is less a direct style than an aggressive one, in the sense that it gives no advantage to those who make use of it, except where the provocation is very obvious. In this situation, provocation is more closely associated with dispute or confrontation.

The provocative style in a company is usually marginal as it requires a high degree of self confidence and a strong capacity for accepting the criticism or rejection of others. It demands recklessness rather than courage, as it does not establish a relationship on equal footing which is a characteristic of a relationship based on courage.

CONVICTION is a deliberate attitude and is extremely important to initiative taking. It derives from the principle 'I want to because I believe'. The style of initiative which results from this is demonstrative, seeking to convince, to set the example.

It is a prophetic style: 'Let's act this way, the consequences will be this and this, as they should be.'

In companies this style is widely used by bosses. Their powerful beliefs and/or will to succeed disguise their lack of deep personal desire which leads them to function on the basis of sound but rigid principles.

Others use this style of initiative but add a dimension of proselytism. This translates simply but powerfully as 'I'm doing it, those who love me, follow me'.

Finally the most pro-active attitude on the spectrum representing styles of initiative is initiative through DESIRE or WANT.

It is plainly illustrated in the simple, frank expression of what you want which then translates into direct action: 'I want, I take'. In society and more so in companies this immediacy or proximity between desire and action with the purpose of obtaining the object of desire has always been forbidden and still is.

The 'I want' has yielded way to 'we want', the royal we, but less direct.

The expression 'Always think twice before you speak' is also a way of putting distance between desire and satisfaction.

However, if I want a chocolate ice cream, I don't have to explain or justify myself; and if the ice cream van is close by, I'll go and buy one and eat it with pleasure, especially if it's good.

The 'right to have desires' has been killed off in companies and in society in its broadest sense. We can well see the need for such a move; if it were only necessary to want in order to take, this would become positively dangerous, for the rules of society and laws do not allow for active self expression of all desires. But by acting this way have we not thrown out the baby with the bath water?

When we examine the most successful achievements, they often came about through a desire which manifested itself in an initiative which was socially acceptable, though not always totally so, but which ended up by finding or creating a place for itself.

The initiative to create a business around an idea, for example.

The initiative through INTEREST derives to a lesser degree from the same logic.

The initiative to open supermarkets on Sundays is associated with the interests of the manager and possibly with those of the employees receiving a higher rate of pay, and all this under the guise of the need of the customer to do his shopping on that day.

The more an initiative is based on a desire the clearer it is. In any case it will often be necessary to dress it up as we have seen, in more socially acceptable attributes or justifications, disguising the sources of personal interest in the collective interest.

✎ EXAMINE YOUR STYLE OF INITIATIVE

Think about an initiative you have recently taken. It can be an insignificant or important action. Briefly describe this initiative:

Is this initiative of the Pro-active ❏
or Reactive type? ❏

If it is Pro-active, is it in the style of:
Provocation? ❏
Conviction? ❏
Desire or interest? ❏

If it is Reactive is it in the style of :
Need, necessity? ❏
Dispute? ❏
Rebellion? ❏

Did it achieve its objective?

What contributed to its outcome? (Whether failure or success)

PROPOSITION FOR ANALYSIS: the example you chose is not in itself conclusive nor significant. However, your analysis of it allows you to work out your dominant style for taking the initiative, either through similarity to the example under consideration or through differences from it.
Perhaps you feel that your chosen example is marginal to your usual way of acting. It is possible on the other hand that you clearly recognize this as your usual dominant style of taking initiatives. Finally, it is probable that the chosen example corresponds to a common attitude of yours but that you also have other dominant or secondary styles. It is important to consider this subjectively, but you might also dare to confirm the truth of it with your professional or personal circles. This kind of feed-back often proves useful when you are trying to improve your performance.

TAKING INITIATIVES

TAKING INITIATIVES (X) FUNCTION OF MULTIPLE FACTORS

$$x = f(P,I,C)$$

or

x(Taking initiatives), P (Personality, I (Intentions),
C (Circumstances).
Each style of taking initiatives is linked to an individual's
personality, intentions and circumstances.

PERSONALITY ··········▶ ⎫
INTENTIONS ··········▶ ⎬ INITIATIVES ··········▶ I MPACT
CIRCUMSTANCES ······▶ ⎭

Section 6
TAKING INITIATIVES –
WHAT ARE THE BARRIERS?

There is an old saying that goes: 'Nobody needs to hope in order to venture, nor to succeed in order to persevere'. The driving forces of initiative are varied, sometimes buried in profound motivations of the individual, sometimes much closer to the surface and answering immediate needs.

Faced with all these mainsprings of initiative we should be amazed and even dismayed that so few initiatives are actually taken when the need for them, as we have seen, is so great. It's a fact that forces of opposition do exist; human nature is such that what forces people to act is often hindered by other factors which should be acknowledged not underestimated.

On the contrary, reflection is desirable. The pros and cons should be examined before a decision is made; nor is it a matter of turning these barriers into a comfortable pretext for not taking action.

Recognizing these barriers to initiative helps to remove them, in other words, to act on the possible constraints, on the fears and to liberate oneself from them.

MISSING FACTORS

1. Lack of knowledge
Lack of initiative is not directly linked to lack of knowledge. People who take initiatives do so more often on the basis of intuition or hunches than on concrete knowledge. However, the majority of individuals feel that if they don't have the necessary knowledge to act, it's too risky to do so, and depending on the circumstances, they remain in this state or they acquire the necessary knowledge before venturing any further.

Where knowledge is concerned, we must distinguish two significant factors which do not necessarily correspond to the same type of constraint. A lack of knowledge in the sense of competence, of knowing and know-how could be considered as a deficiency influencing the 'how to do' and thus diminishing the capacity for initiative.

For example, if I am not a specialist technician in a particular area, I will not take the initiative of repairing faulty equipment, but would instead take the initiative of calling a repair man and perhaps when faced with the difficulties of getting one (which is often the case), I would end up resorting to a manual in order to be able to intervene myself.

But lack of knowledge may also cover another aspect: a lack of vision for the future, of not knowing what we are letting ourselves in for once we have taken the initiative. This lack of knowledge is more similar to another barrier which we will deal with later, fear of the unknown. It does not involve the 'how to do' like the previous one, but a lack of confidence and primarily self-confidence. For example I will not take the initiative to enter into conflict with somebody unless I feel sufficiently sure of myself to endure the consequences.

However, it is by confronting this person that I can transcend my fear. It is a vicious circle which I have to break in order to be free from it.

Whereas learning, education and training may remove the barriers of lack of practical knowledge, a lack of confidence is more complex to deal with. There are, however, two phases: on the one hand experience, meaning attempting, and, on the other hand, confrontation of the 'other' in a general way, and of representatives of authority (parents, teachers, bosses...), in particular.

2. Lack of information

Lack of initiative is often due to lack of information. In a way, this is similar to the previous aspect discussed, but whereas lack of knowledge, as we have seen, concerns know-how, the barrier associated with lack of information corresponds more simply with the fact that we are lacking a piece of data, some information, fact or opinion and that this deficiency prevents us taking an initiative.

For example, I would happily have taken the initiative of going to meet my friend upon his arrival at the airport, but I don't know the flight number or time of arrival and I can't get hold of anyone to give me this information. Of course, I should

Personal notes

What, in your opinion, are the main barriers to taking initiatives?

_____

_____

_____

_____

_____

_____

_____

_____

_____

_____

_____

_____

_____

_____

have thought of this earlier but it was only a postponed appointment that made me think of it.

Lack of information is only a temporary barrier to initiative. It involves urgent circumstances or at least situations where acquiring the necessary information is impossible, or temporarily unavailable, but this does not make it a permanent barrier. It could, however, be enough to stop actions taking place, to miss appointments or lose business.

Taking the initiative to put out a fire and evacuate the premises implies knowledge of the whereabouts of the fire extinguisher and the fire exits. Being in possession of information is fundamentally important, the example of security or fire procedures is an essential one from the first day an employee arrives in the job.

3. Lack of desire

No initiative will exist without the minimum requirement of desire. Lacking desire is fatal for taking initiatives. When the desire is not strong enough the tendency for all of us is to get distracted and fail to achieve our goals. You stop en route on some pretext or other and what could have been an initiative gets thrown on to the scrap heap of tries, attempts and other expressions of indecision.

Another facet of the lack of desire is expressed in a lack of interest for the problem or situation. The person is not sufficiently stimulated to be spurred into action and prefers to wait. At the time of redundancy plans, certain arrangements involve an inducement from the outset in the form of money accompanying a request for resignation or voluntary redundancy. The initiative to leave for some people will be based on the sum offered to them, in other words their own direct interests. Within one company, a number of cases may be dealt with over a period, during which time the sum in question may increase significantly.

FEARS

1. Fear of confrontation

Initiative requires a certain courage. In particular this courage is expressed in relationships by confrontation.

It may appear perfectly natural to most of us to argue, to exchange ideas and to confront others, but it often happens that a confrontational situation becomes unpleasant or uncomfortable and creates a real barrier.

We have all experienced this type of reaction but some people are more susceptible to it. The result is a difficulty in taking initiatives.

For example, at a restaurant I would not take the initiative of sending back a wine which has corked unless I felt comfortable about confronting the wine waiter, otherwise I would drink my wine, perhaps even down to the sediment.

2. Fear of the unknown

One of the most powerful barriers to taking initiatives is fear of the unknown. Within a company, not knowing where you're going is an essential reason for ceasing to proceed any further, and with good reason. However, few know what will become of the company in the medium term. Here we have a paradoxical situation, for curiously enough, it is often inertia, the normal pace and force of habit which ensure the possibility of taking initiatives.

Philosophically, it is because you know that anything is possible, that you can take initiatives, but it's also because not everything is possible all at once, that initiatives are worth taking.

3. Fear of the obstacles to be overcome

Sometimes you don't feel on top of the task to be accomplished. The road seems too long, the problems too overwhelming. This sentiment is also an inhibitor, the result of which is to eliminate any will to act, meaning that the initiative is no longer conceivable for you and is pointless. For example, feeling powerless to convince somebody reputed to be stubborn and authoritarian will block the initiative of those who have to do it.

Climbing Everest is an exploit which demonstrates that it is possible to overcome what appear to be insurmountable obstacles. But beyond the practice, the preparation and the will to succeed, Chris Bonnington must deep down inside really have believed it was possible.

This sentiment is evidently not shared by everyone, when faced either with Everest or with other problems. It is for this reason that heroes and achievers of this kind receive so many messages of thanks, as if their exploits rekindle hope or confidence in those who have lost it.

4. Fear of losing

Nobody likes losing. A fear of losing can also be a barrier to initiative in that it is the fear of not accomplishing, of not succeeding.

Failure is felt as a bitter experience by some people. In order to avoid the situation they would prefer not to act at all ('When in doubt, don't', as the proverb advises) and thus not take the risk of losing.

Repeated failure can even be the basis for pathological behaviour when faced with taking initiatives. Reactions provoked by conditioned reflexes are founded on these principles. For those who systematically fail it ends up as a syndrome which inhibits, partially or totally, their capacity to take initiatives.

5. Fear of winning

In contrast to the fear of losing, we also encounter a more rare but still classic barrier among sporting personalities and in all forms of competition, the fear of winning. We've all witnessed the problems for a tennis player on the brink of winning a match, who suddenly loses control of his skills and finds it impossible to take the initiatives necessary to conclude the match.

These barriers to initiative demonstrate that the range of constraints is a broad one, made up of a multitude of conscious and unconscious elements which are not easily overcome. Knowing what they are is the first step towards release, towards the aptitude for taking initiatives by reducing, even eliminating these difficulties.

TRACE THE BARRIERS TO YOUR INITIATIVES

For each type of barrier presented, find an example which concerns you personally and describe it clearly.

Analyze your barriers to initiatives by subsequently responding to the following questions:

Has the barrier been removed? If so, how? If not, why not? What could you have done, or what can you do, to make these initiatives easier?

Type of barrier	Examples	Barrier removed Yes/no	How?/Why?
LACK OF KNOWLEDGE			
LACK OF INFORMATION			
LACK OF DESIRE			
FEAR OF CONFRONTATION			
FEAR OF THE UNKNOWN			
FEAR OF OBSTACLES			
FEAR OF LOSING			
FEAR OF WINNING			

61

A THOUSAND AND ONE WAYS OF STIFLING INITIATIVE

Besides an *individual's* multiple personal barriers to initiative, a *company,* over the course of its development may, in a number of ways and means, actually reduce or even veto signs of initiative through precaution or fear. A company can become unintentionally a master of the art of preventing initiative.

The following examples represent a sample of these methods which, if not overtly recommended, are practised by the individual and by the company and whose effect is to discourage initiative.

1. Uniformity

Getting the individual used to the norm, and considering all employees to be exactly the same as each other, without distinction or individuality, is an extremely efficient method of annihilating any desire for initiative. With the exception of some extraordinary individuals, standardization creates a lack of motivation and a passive attitude.

2. Blind obedience, submission

The management style is certainly a critical factor for subordinates, but the means of subordination also has an effect on the hierarchy. Stanley Milgram has shown in his study on submission to authority that the critical mind and the capacity to react to a situation imposed by authority are relatively weak. This submissive attitude is evidently a root cause of avoiding initiative.

3. Terror

Creating a climate of terror by constantly threatening everyone's actions or decisions is another means of killing off initiative. We noticed earlier that threats are more inhibiting than punishment, which are reacted to as either just or unjust. Threats, however, inhibit the action from the outset.

4. Pre-satisfied Desires

The origin of desire is still poorly understood, but it is clear that by denying any possibility of a desire being realized, the child or individual has difficulty in maintaining the expression of his desire. Nevertheless, in an even more obvious way, the child who sees his desires pre-satisfied, meaning that one anticipates everything he could want, risks losing the sense of desire quickly. But desire is necessarily at the origin of initiative. To pre-satisfy is thus one more way of killing initiative.

WHAT HAPPENS IN YOUR COMPANY TO KILL OFF INITIATIVE?

Illustrate each of these practices through personal example or one encountered in your company. Also ask yourself the following questions:
What is or was the impact? Who does it suit or did it suit, in other words who benefits or benefited from it? What solution was found or did you suggest?

Ways of killing initiative	Examples	Impact	Beneficiary	Solution
UNIFORMITY				
SUBMISSION				
TERROR				
PRE-SATISFIED DESIRE				
CERTAINTY				
LAX ATTITUDE				
IGNORANCE				
LACK OF APRECIATION				
OTHER				

5. Certainty

Taking initiatives implies a risk, once we introduce certainty then the feeling of risk disappears. If we are sure of succeeding there is nothing at stake and thus no desire or need. On the other hand, if we are sure we won't succeed, what's the point of taking the initiative?

6. Lax Attitude

In no demands are made on him or if he cannot relate to the context, the individual is not stimulated except in exceptional cases. Initiative is subjected to a sort of indifference and appeals to an individual to take the initiative are not made. The lax attitude permitting such indifference rapidly kills off initiative.

7. Ignorance, lacking information

Not educating or informing is a particularly effective means of killing off initiative. If an individual is uninformed of the situation he won't know what to react to. Furthermore, it is not easy to desire something we don't know about. Ignorance is a fermenting agent for passivity and non-existence of initiative.

8. Lack of Appreciation

Emphasizing bad initiatives or not recognizing good ones seriously diminishes the faculty for taking initiatives. One of two things can happen in such circumstances; either the person lacks autonomy and quickly finds only obstacles to his initiatives, or he possesses sufficient autonomy and will look elsewhere for appreciation of his initiatives. In both cases the company has killed off, if not the initiative then at least the benefits to be gained from it.

Section 7
WHAT ARE THE TECHNIQUES FOR TAKING INITIATIVES?

The techniques already described for taking initiatives refer to what we see happening in companies. Some are recommended, others should only be used with caution and advice, others should be disregarded.

The illustration below shows how unwise it would be to adopt all available techniques without first becoming fully aware of the consequences and implications of such actions. Learn to distinguish between things which seem immediately effective and those which are long term, what is moral and what is not.

At the end of the section you will be asked to respond to questions on each of the eight techniques for taking initiatives.

65

EIGHT TECHNIQUES

Technique 1 – Talking about the problem as if a solution is possible

The fable of the fox and the grapes shows us that all too often desire diminishes because the obstacle appears to us insurmountable, whereas if we believe the objective to be attainable, we dare, and in many cases we manage to modify the crux of the problem sufficiently to create a new situation.

Let's not forget that within a system, the modification of one element affects the others as the balance is readjusted.

We have known for a long time that belief – whether in a Supreme Being or simply in what you want – is likely to encourage the taking of initiatives. 'God helps those who help themselves' is one famous example. In any case, we're not suggesting you force a belief on yourself which would have little effect anyway, but that you seek discussion (with a colleague, boss or friend) on the subject occupying your thoughts in order to render it more familiar, more concrete and more attainable.

Technique 2 – the umbrella

We often want to limit the risks before taking an initiative. So we surround ourselves with precautionary measures knowing that it is not possible to anticipate every eventuality. But if it is unnecessary to open an umbrella when it is not raining, it is still prudent to carry one if rain is forecast, which suggests that no move can be made without 'getting your feet wet'.

Far be it from us to advocate automatically putting up an umbrella, which would be in direct contradiction with the idea of promoting initiative, but to whet your appetite for initiatives it is preferable to get a few successes under your belt in the first attempts. This is an obvious principle for any kind of training or education. It is also recommended that you first reconnoitre the terrain and analyze the existing pressures. Sometimes it will even be necessary to retreat to achieve a better result.

Technique 3 – The fait accompli

The technique of the fait accompli advocates disobedience, subversion, even sedition. In a company, this attitude of 'no turning back' is rarely forgiven, even if the result is a positive one, after-effects will remain and latent distrust will tarnish relations.

It may appear to be easier to act first and explain later but it only looks that way. Initiative does not exclude information or dialogue unless of course it only concerns yourself.

However, this is common practice in companies. It is often found in individuals who prefer to function independently.

Note that we are not talking about a crisis situation where we have to take decisions and act without the possibility of consultation or dialogue, but a situation where the employee decides on principle to favour the fait accompli.

Technique 4 – Overwhelming information

When a system is inflexible, in other words, where there are only limited possibilities for taking initiatives, where the disciplinary code and procedures are very strict and the supervision a constraint, the objective then becomes one of creating a zone of autonomy.

A means of gaining room to manoeuvre is to shower your superiors and colleagues with information. While they are occupied with sorting out the useful from the superfluous information, initiatives can be established. Take these initiatives after informing those who ought to know about them. Certainly the risks are great, especially if you fail, but you enable development to take place in the system. By applying its rigid logic, you exploit its weaknesses and show up its limitations.

This is a case of an attitude which should only be envisaged after all other possible solutions have been sought out through healthy communication paths, but in cases of urgency or necessity this method proves most effective.

Beware! Any time this is attempted outside a rigid context such as we have described, it is viewed as self-exclusive, a challenge to authority and a search for independence on the part of the one who launches the move. Obviously this will be regarded as undesirable from the company's point of view.

Technique 5 – Prepare: making the initiative less dangerous

What often makes initiative dangerous is the element of surprise, sometimes even the feeling of short-circuiting. By informing people of your intentions wherever possible, this risk is curtailed.

On the other hand, when surprise is vital to the success of an initiative, it is by using the element of surprise to its maximum effect that we will diminish the risk.

Another method of minimizing risk as regards taking an initiative, is by anticipating the consequences. Obviously nobody can predict every eventuality that could crop up, but it is a matter of being prepared to explain your choices, decisions and actions, as much in a situation of success as of failure.

Technique 6 – Temporary block
Lack of initiative may be associated with a lack of will or desire. We fall into a sort of lethargy or at least a kind of passivity which comforts itself with the question 'what's the point?', justifying idleness.

So it is a case of breaking out of this attitude of resignation and re-discovering an active attitude leading to initiative.

The technique of the temporary block often allows this objective to be achieved.

This consists of deciding that a certain action, gesture or aptitude is suddenly rendered impossible, unusable and unworkable over a given period (an hour, a day, a week), according to the imaginary block.

By the end of the given period and often before it, the need or desire will have re-surfaced. But it will not only be a need for the 'forbidden' action or gesture, but of others too which have cropped up in connection with it and which create new needs.

Technique 7 – Getting your colleagues used to it
It is all the more difficult to take initiatives when your colleagues are unaccustomed to seeing you take them. So they may adopt a system of resistance. But if, on the other hand, they are used to your surprises, and your initiatives are known and recognized, you have created a chink in the system which is just waiting for more initiatives from you.

However, beware of falling into the trap of having the others depend on you, the eventual consequence of which would be in the end to inhibit their initiatives and create a relationship of unequal footing. As we have seen, this balance and alternation of initiatives is beneficial to a healthy development of the company.

Technique 8 – Anticipation
The basic idea of this lies in knowing how to use the opponent's force or movement as in certain Japanese martial art forms such as Hakido. In a more general sense, in all sports or arts, it is a matter of using the 'voids' which actually represent for the experts, breathing spaces or platforms

for anticipating the obstacle or the next move in the sequence of action. Initiative takes its force from anticipation. So in practice it can operate on the basis of flexibility, diversion or the lever effect.

These technical terms borrowed from sporting or at least physical exploits, find an equivalent in the area of relationships and in company life.

Anticipation within a company involves listening out for and observing everything which may constitute information. Such are the foundations of initiative in this context. Using one's intelligence to modify what one has heard, plus a modicum of common sense, gives us what is normally called 'intuition'. This intuition can never simply be put down to chance or an unexpected stroke of luck; it is the conclusion of a blend of elements which may be lengthy or rapid but which permits initiatives to be taken with confidence.

You will recognize by a few words, gestures or expressions when the time is right for avoiding pitfalls, aborting unhelpful conversations, reviving important subjects, ignoring red herrings or confronting attacks or attempts at dissuasion.

Easy to say! Fine in theory, but in practice it requires great effort, precision and training.

HOW DO WE TRAIN OURSELVES TO ANTICIPATE?

Anticipation is more of an art than a technique. Above all it is the capacity to observe; this observation involves general human reactions but also individual peculiarities.

Human reactions may, to some extent, be considered a logical, traditional and near-mechanical pattern. In reality the range of reactions to a stimulus is very limited, even if the mode of expressing these reactions is specific to each person. This is how we can predict what someone is going to do, how we can compile statistics on purchasing behaviour, public protection or public savings.

Observation and experience bring together these elements which it is then possible to integrate into future decisions.

But these general reactions are not enough. For one thing, they evolve with time and differ according to cultures and geography. They are characteristics which cannot be changed, even if some do seem like innate reflexes.

Observation of individual peculiarities and situations is more complex. It is a case of making use of the senses in order to first take in and subsequently to interpret the information. But often our senses deceive us, and lead us to make mistakes (projections, rejections and all other manner of psychological phenomena which interfere). The temptation to put comprehension before feeling is a strong one. Turner, the painter used to say 'I paint what I see, not what I know'.

The search for comfort, security and stability leads us to cling to what we know, a major handicap to listening. Among the instruments which facilitate the art of anticipation, four are worth emphasizing.

– Prepare without being inflexible
Preparing for an action represents only part of the classic recommendations for removing obstacles or for warning those concerned. But be careful not to kill what is alive in a relationship by over rigid preparation. You cannot foresee every eventuality, and people's reactions in particular, but it is possible to know that there will be some.

Anticipation doesn't only involve foreseeing these reactions but also sometimes provoking them. Thus it allows us to better analyze and interpret them without surprise or embarrassment. The success of improvised comedy and theatre is obviously due to the talent of the actors who, as well as having a text to deliver, also play to the audience's reactions and endeavour to provoke and stimulate them.

To train yourself to anticipate is to employ plausible hypotheses, linked to behaviour you have already seen, and make use of them in order to act.

– Listen to the little words
'You have once again overlooked the secondary effects...'
'You have nearly achieved your objective... or almost succeeded in your mission...'

There are scores of examples to demonstrate that the only words heard by the person being spoken to are 'again', 'nearly', or 'almost'. These serve to qualify the impact of the phrase but radically change the sense of it.

The little words are tools for interpreting or even decoding relationships. Anticipation involves reacting to each one of them in order to formulate hypotheses on their significance and choose the most appropriate among them.

– Discover the hidden significance
Every phrase or expression can disguise a different meaning. The

EVALUATE YOUR SENSE OF MORALITY AND YOUR EFFICIENCY IN TAKING INITIATIVES

From the list of techniques for taking initiatives, determine those which seem to you the most effective and assign each of them the symbol corresponding to their moral value in your opinion. Use the following:

– –	completely amoral
–	not moral
+	acceptable
++	Totally moral

Techniques	Moral Value
MAKING IT SEEM POSSIBLE	
THE UMBRELLA	
THE FAIT ACCOMPLI	
OVERWHELMING INFORMATION	
MAKING THE INITIATIVE LESS DANGEROUS	
TEMPORARY BLOCK	
GETTING YOUR COLLEAGUES USED TO IT	
ANTICIPATION	

Which of these techniques do you use most frequently?

71

words, obviously, have definite meanings, but the way they are used can alter them. Those which we use intentionally, tinged with politeness are thus pre-coded (hallo, goodbye, please, you're welcome). The tone, gesture or expression, however, can alter or even reverse the implication of the words, not to mention the slip of the tongue, or other manifestations of the unconscious.

Without getting psychoanalytical about it, hearing these expressions gives us a chance to work out their meaning.

Learning to anticipate means seeking to understand the hidden meaning of the words and language.

– Juxtaposing or superimposing words and acts to compare them

You can define a person's credibility as the compatibility which exists between what he says and what he does, between his words and his deeds.

Any discrepancy is a source of discredit and that is why we often find various expressions like: 'do as you say and say as you do', as a value or principle of behaviour in many company projects and management charters.

Taking note of these disparities by comparing word and deed is also learning to anticipate. This allows us to understand and determine more clearly our course of action according to the consistency and credibility of whoever we're dealing with.

Section 8
TECHNIQUES ENCOURAGING PEOPLE TO TAKE INITIATIVES

Can we make people take initiatives? Yes, it is possible, but not just anybody or at any time.

We all have a basic positive or negative view of human nature. We either consider the individual as fundamentally being a waster, or on the other hand, as being interested in all kinds of activities. If the first is true, we must suppose that the individual is unlikely to take initiatives, whereas his counterpart in the second instance probably will. Other theories might lead us to divide the world into two categories: those who can take initiatives and the rest.

These generalized and simplistic classifications do not promote a motivating vision for getting people to take initiatives.

We have seen that taking initiatives is linked to the personality, intentions and circumstances. A desire to act based on this premiss implies a regard for the individual as a unique being and seeks to draw out the best he has to offer, both for his own and the company's benefit.

Beware! The temptation to manipulate, which implies getting somebody to do something without their being aware of it, does not come under our heading 'encouraging people to take initiatives'. Other books deal with this but our purpose, without taking a holier than thou attitude, is the opposite to this practice, simply a concern for long term efficiency.

Manipulation can only develop inhibition and an incapacity for taking initiatives in its victims.

Furthermore, it is a weapon which can only be used once; when the victim sees through it, he loses confidence for good in whoever has manipulated him.

As in all management actions, getting people to take initiatives involves arousing the individual's interest, and not just blindly tacking on to him some theory or practice on the pretext that it would have worked with others. You can't get just anybody to take any old initiative. This, as we have already seen, would be senseless. All we can do is create a favourable climate and tap into relationships which promise the potential for initiative.

Setting a good example is not a technique in itself but, in many cases, showing the example of taking initiatives will have a stimulating influence on the transmission of this capacity to others, if not immediately, then in the long term. Taking initiatives yourself is an essential incentive for all the techniques presented in this chapter.

SIX TECHNIQUES FOR STIMULATING INITIATIVE

1. Setting up limited choice situations

This technique consists of playing the situation so that the field of choice is reduced to its simplest form of expression and the initiative appears to be an alternative.

The alternative is a practice that sales representatives are well acquainted with, in order to narrow the field of choice for their customers. The apparent choice remains the customer's own but from a selection narrowed down to two.

The 'back against the wall' method goes a step further by confronting the person with an apparent obligation. The line of reasoning goes like this: I've no other choice but to do something, and get some benefit from it, or even set it up as my own idea by making it my initiative.

This technique works on the feeling of self-determination of choices: 'I want to have the choice of my choices'.

2. Making them think

Getting people to take initiatives means getting them to think, getting them to stop depending on others, to

> ## THE RANGE OF TECHNIQUES
> ## FOR GETTING PEOPLE TO TAKE INITIATIVES
>
> SETTING UP LIMITED CHOICE SITUATIONS
> MAKING THEM THINK
> ASSIGNING MISSIONS
> LAYING DOWN THE RULES OF THE GAME
> EVALUATING INITIATIVES
> DEVELOPING 'AUTONOMY'

stop meekly complying for the sake of a quiet life and to stop worrying what others think.

It is by getting them into the habit of thinking, by constantly inciting reflection, by demanding it right from the outset of a relationship with someone, that we generate initiative. Time is a delicate element here as it isn't easy to pinpoint the exact moment when initiative will begin to manifest itself.

This technique works on our need for recognition for our intelligence and contribution to decisions.

3. Assigning missions

Every activity may be considered in two different ways depending on the manner in which it has been presented to you. Either you are dealing with a specific task bearing no direct relation whatsoever to your environment, or you will be in a situation where you will know the origins, reasons and aims of the proposed activity, so that there is at least a link established with the motive even if the motivation has yet to surface.

Thus, the washing up is a task which has to be done, signifying that obligation is the underlying reason for this activity. But doing the dishes could also be an assignment entrusted to a group of boy scouts with the objective of completing it in under five minutes without breaking a single thing. Almost any task can be transformed into a mission. Motivating in this instance consists above all else of giving a motive.

Initiatives start with this notion of a mission which implies an action plus responsibility whereas the task only demands obedience and execution without thinking.

This technique acts on the feeling of gratitude based on the element of trust.

4. Laying down the rules of the game

Initiative is possible because the rules of the game are laid down and known. Without these rules everything may be envisaged but direction is lacking.

This is expressed within companies by inconsistent behaviour which we cannot even term deviant as nobody knows which direction is the right one.

Knowing the rules of the game, in other words, the structure and normal procedures in the company, gives rise to the confidence necessary for taking initiatives.

Note that when triggering initiative, it is the critical faculty which is stimulated. This being so, we can expect to see the rules of the game brought into question by the people who are using them. But isn't this challenging a type of progress? Yesterday's rules won't necessarily be tomorrow's, and those who develop them are doubtless the same people who use them and perceive their limitations.

This technique acts on the feeling of security necessary for taking initiatives.

5. Evaluating initiatives

When evaluating employee performance it is essential to recognize the importance of initiative taking and to acknowledge and reward it.

However, the question which crops up when you try to evaluate initiatives is that of evaluation criteria.

Certainly, the number of initiatives taken by an employee will serve as an indicator but their quality and relevance should also be taken into account.

These initiatives must, of course, conform to company objectives in the short, medium or long term. Actual results of initiatives taken should be assessed and the employee concerned given feedback.

For instance, the evaluation of initiatives could be made part of a review meeting, focusing on their frequency, originality, relevance and effect.

This technique relies on giving an employee recognition for their initiatives and aids communication and understanding between employees and managers.

ASSESS YOUR ABILITY FOR ENCOURAGING PEOPLE TO TAKE INITIATIVES

Consult your professional (boss, colleagues, team) and personal contacts (partner, children, friends) and elicit their opinion on the following questions:
– Do they think you stimulate the taking of initiatives?
– In their opinion, what techniques do you use?
Compare their responses with your perceptions.

Techniques	Professional environment	Personal environment
SETTING UP LIMITED CHOICE SITUATIONS		
MAKING THEM THINK		
ASSIGNING MISSIONS		
DRAWING UP THE RULES OF THE GAME		
EVALUATING INITIATIVES		
DEVELOPING 'AUTONOMY'		

6. Developing 'autonomy'

In the case of initiative, just like anything else, it is difficult to turn a lame horse into a champion racehorse. Temperament and education play an essential role. Also, before seeking to modify or improve an individual's capacity for initiative, it is preferable to start by developing existing potential; that is, a degree of real autonomy on which to build an aptitude for initiative.

In particular a company whose objectives and strategies involve a high level of change will have to integrate in its recruitment criteria notions of adaptability and potential, rather than focus in a restrictive manner on technical skills and immediate operational aspects.

This technique depends on the adaptability of people for changing situations.

TEN SITUATIONS STIMULATING INITIATIVE

There is an entire spectrum of possibilities for stimulating initiative, but to achieve the right result, it is necessary to use the appropriate strokes and adapt them to the situation and the person we're dealing with.

Here are some strokes we can apply to incite initiative which will bring great benefits.

1. A problem

Inciting initiative is to focus attention on a specific problem. The problem serves as the stimulus; it may not trigger any reaction but in many cases it will create involvement in the person facing the problem.

2. A desire

Creating desire is, one of the roles of advertising and marketing. The initiative of buying is studied in profound detail, so that the average or well-informed consumer can buy with more confidence.

3. A belief

Even though the approach of this guide is essentially rational, it also places value on people's beliefs.

WHAT INITIATIVE-INCITING SITUATIONS DO YOU USE?

From the ten situations inciting initiative, which are those you most willingly use?
Shade or fill in that part of the area 0 – 5 which corresponds to your inclination (0 very little use, 5 strong use of the situation).

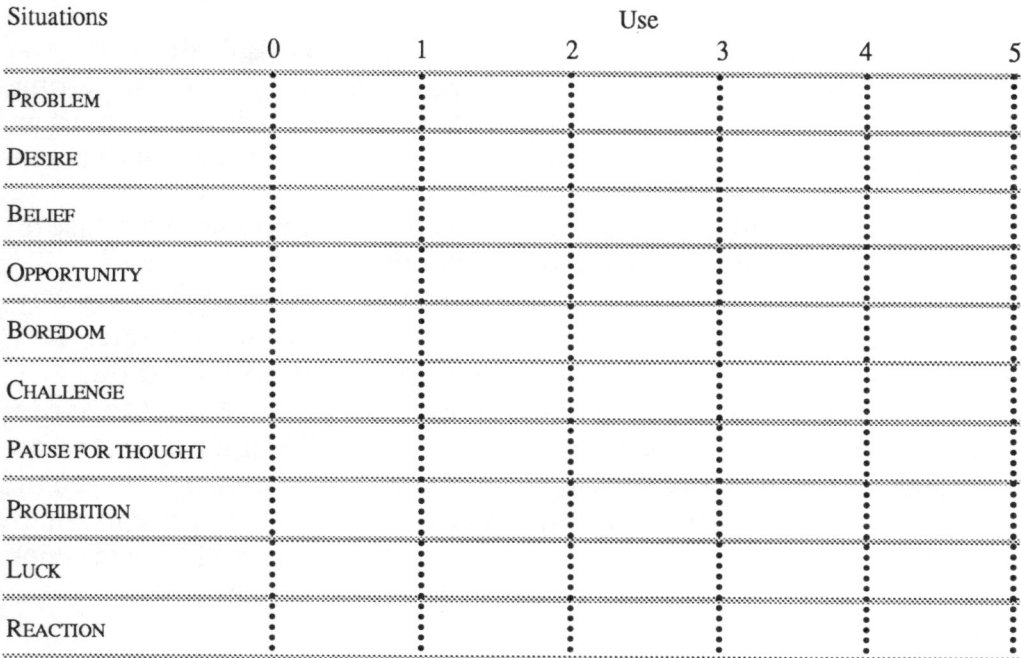

Situations	0	1	2	Use 3	4	5
PROBLEM						
DESIRE						
BELIEF						
OPPORTUNITY						
BOREDOM						
CHALLENGE						
PAUSE FOR THOUGHT						
PROHIBITION						
LUCK						
REACTION						

Interpretation of results: if your predominant areas are

PROBLEM OR PAUSE FOR THOUGHT	You try to emphasize a rational approach to taking initiatives.
OPPORTUNITY, REACTION, BOREDOM, CHALLENGE	You try to play on the emotional forces as much as the rational to get people to take initiatives.
DESIRE, BELIEF, CHANCE, PROHIBITION	You stress the emotional approach to taking initiatives.

Those most likely to get others to take initiatives use the entire range, but everyone always has certain dominant strokes which enhance his chances of success.

Those who find support or even guidance in a theory, doctrine or belief, are often led to take initiatives. These people are often more in tune with the beliefs of their doctrine than with the objectives of the company because they firmly believe in what they are doing.

Our critical faculties are an instrument of initiative and particularly in the case of beliefs.

4. An opportunity

It is opportunity which makes the thief as long as he takes his chance. Provoking opportunities means creating conditions where more initiatives can be taken.

5. Boredom

Boredom can also play a part in initiative taking. Placing people in boring, stagnant situations can provoke a desire to get out of this state and thus take initiatives.

6. Challenge

Challenging someone to get something done can also be a method of stimulating initiative in many cases. However, it doesn't work as often as we may think.

It is preferable to issue challenges sparingly and with prudence, but as long as it is justly applied, this method could cause some surprises.

7. Pause for thought

A need for reflection is imposed by asking leading questions and pushing the person to seek consistency, which will lead to the conclusion that the only way to achieve this consistency and avoid ambiguity and error is to go into action. This will lead to an initiative being taken.

8. Prohibition (disobedience)

Paradox also plays a role in setting provocative restrictions, in other words, ones which make us want to break them.

This is particularly so in the case of children.

However, beware of the two-way guilt trips this can generate. It is indispensable to talk about this disobedience if we want to avoid accidents. We mustn't let it be believed that we have been duped by this disobedience nor pretend not to see it. Perhaps we will have to adopt a new system of rules.

9. Luck

A particular form of belief consists of believing in your lucky star or in a stroke of fortune. Feeling that you're on a winning streak can be the opportunity to incite initiative but beware, with luck it is often a case of easy come, easy go.

WHO SHALL WE GET TO TAKE THE INITIATIVE?

Who would you like to see taking initiatives?

Persons concerned	Name	Reasons
EMPLOYEES		
COLLEAGUES		
BOSS		
PARTNER		
CHILDREN		
RELATIVES		
FRIENDS		
CLIENTS		
SUPPLIERS		

What have you done up to now to get them to take initiatives?

What can you draw on from the list for conducting initiatives?

Problem	❏	Desire	❏	Belief	❏
Opportunity	❏	Boredom	❏	Challenge	❏
Pause for thought	❏	Prohibition	❏	Reaction	❏

10. Reaction

Finally, telling lies in order to discover fact, playing devil's advocate or simply affirming something to provoke a reaction is a widely used means of releasing initiative when it doesn't seem to be finding expression of its own accord.

FOUR APPROACHES TO LEARNING INITIATIVE

Educating and making those around us capable of taking initiatives is an everyday activity. Whether we're talking about children or our colleagues, the principles are still the same.

Great teachers have made their contribution to this notion without any one of them treating it as such.

Here are four summaries of the main approaches to this subject.

Socrates

Socrates' theories apply perfectly to the development of the ability for taking initiatives.

The principle starts from the idea that everybody possesses within himself the knowledge and resources necessary for understanding and especially for progressing. All we have to do is ask the questions which will make him think and he will draw his own conclusions without anyone having to teach them to him.

It is likely that this method meets its limitations in the area of the sciences; discovering the theories of quantum physics in this way seems improbable, as well as for all disciplines involving rules such as law or foreign languages; Socrates' theories will find little response in those who have no learning.

But for initiative, Socrates is a good guide.

If we want to 'teach initiative', we must focus on the student and, by means of questions or situations, lead him to react until he perceives his method of working, begins to ask himself questions and undertakes actions on his own; in other words, until he learns to take initiatives.

DO YOU PUT EDUCATIONAL APPROACHES INTO ACTION?

Have you ever practised any educational approaches similar to those we have described?

ON WHOM?	WITH WHAT RESULTS?

Suggest other educational approaches likely to develop initiative in those you deal with.

O'Neil (Free children of Summerhill)
The methods advocated by O'Neil and adopted by many therapists, such as Bruno Bettelheim, starts with the idea that it is norms, rules and restrictions which limit a child's capacity for expressing his desires. As the latter are the driving force of initiative, we must create a permissive, open environment, likely to promote the undertaking of actions and to highlight these actions rather than criticizing or ignoring them.

What applies to children with difficulties (autistic, in care)finds its equivalent at the heart of the company, among integrated individuals, in management modes.

Creating a stimulating context where there is a ready ear available, where taking ideas on board is common practice and where initiative is recognized and valued, is a guarantee of the improvement of each person's confidence and development of the capacity for initiative.

Note that such a method does not mean that everything becomes possible; the role of listening is precisely to evaluate what emerges as initiative in line with objectives, and what comes under deviant tendencies or even bad faith.

Freinet
Discovery by doing.
Freinet's basic contribution is to have incorporated practice into the teaching. Nowadays most teachers are familiar with the statistics concerning the capacity for understanding and memorizing involved in the learning process (20 per cent of what we hear, 30 per cent of what we see and 70 per cent of what we do). So it is essential to make practice part of learning, not only by repetition and training but also by discovering what is to be learned.

Giving a child clay enables him to discover its properties and make pottery or sculpture without a model or example likely to inhibit him. The child, by playing with the clay, will discover for himself some things about pottery making, and perhaps also develop interest or even pleasure in this activity. This will give him the desire to continue, to learn the techniques and rules of the art.

Teaching the spirit of initiative passes through a similar procedure. Confronting real, initiative demanding situations, is part of the manager's attitude if he wants to develop this capacity for initiative in his employees. Of course, as with all learning processes, there is room for error and failure which must be

THE TALE OF THE LITTLE PONY WHO LEARNS COURAGE

But initiative also has to do with courage. Can we learn courage? I'm not talking about physical courage here, which perhaps a form of exercise could help us achieve, but courage in relationships which companies and businesses certainly need. Preparing for it means on the one hand, confronting situations, which gives you experience, and on the other, confronting others, which gives you self-confidence.

The Chinese tale of the little pony who crosses the river illustrates what may well be an education in taking initiatives.

The little pony who has to cross the river

The story takes place in a mountain village. Many big, strong horses are working the land. Three of them are hitched to a cart. All three work hard. The white mare has just given birth. The little foal hardly ever leaves his mother's side.

One day, however, his mother sends him to carry a sack of grain to the mill for her. With the sack on his back, the little pony gallops in the direction of the mill. But he comes to a sudden stop! A foaming river blocks his path. What should he do?

On the river bank, an old bull is grazing peacefully. The little pony approaches and asks him:

'Mr Bull, do you think I can get across that river?
– Why yes, of course, the water's not that deep, it only reaches my knees; I crossed it only yesterday'.

But hardly had he dipped the tip of a hoof into the river when a squirrel ran up to him shouting:

'Hey, little pony, don't try to cross there, it is too dangerous! The water is too deep. One of my friends got drowned there yesterday.'

Now our little pony is in trouble. Who does he believe? The bull? The squirrel? Without taking time to think, he does an about turn and gallops home. His mother, astonished to see him back so soon, asks: 'Why are you back already?' The little pony replies, stammering: 'Mr Bull says the river isn't deep and I can easily get across but then a squirrel came up and said just the opposite'. And his mother replies: 'Did you wonder why their stories were so contradictory? Didn't you notice anything?'

His mother continues gently: 'The bull is big and strong, so naturally he finds the water shallow, but the squirrel is so small that he could quite easily drown in a puddle of water. In his eyes, the water is certainly too deep. Each one considers the problem according to his own size. And what about you, have you considered the problem?' All of a sudden, the little pony's mind is clear and he quickly leaves again at a gallop.

When he reaches the river once again, the bull and the squirrel repeat their advice. But this time the little pony has his own ideas. He compares his size to that of both the bull and the squirrel and declares: 'I'm going to try!' He is bigger than the squirrel and smaller than the bull, so for him the river will neither be as deep as the squirrel claims nor as shallow as the bull claims. He attempts the crossing and reaches the other side safely.

Leaving the sack of grain at the mill, he returns home quickly. How nice to hear his mother's words of praise.

Since then, whenever the little pony finds himself faced with a new situation, he never hesitates to ask the advice of others. This means that he always thinks before attempting anything new! Each experience makes him wiser and more resourceful.

What ideas does this story inspire in you? Apply them to your company.

accounted for. But without the opportunity to practise, it is probable that those who possess a good capacity for initiative will not stay, and the others have no chance to acquire any.

Chaplin (The Kid)

In his film *The Kid*, Charlie Chaplin shows us an abandoned child. We see him in deep despair, without food or shelter. It is through need that he will learn about life, that he will find his own solutions, that he will have to take sometimes dangerous and not always legal initiatives, but ones that will help him to stay alive.

We can learn from this that need can be a source of initiative. In more concrete terms, this means that it's not always a good thing to resolve an employee's problems systematically, and that he should approach them head on and be confronted by them himself if we want his experience to be beneficial.

Section 9
EDUCATING EMPLOYEES TO TAKE INITIATIVES

A global training procedure to introduce change in terms of taking initiatives within the ranks of a company may be envisaged in the form of a training session.

Beware, not every company is ready to face up to this type of re-thinking. To succeed in terms of a training plan, to deal with the notion of initiative without too much risk of misunderstanding or whatever, you must have set yourself certain preconditions. In effect, initiative is a notion, as we have seen, which implies that the difference between autonomy and independence must be made clear to everyone. If this is not the case, you will come across attempts at initiative which bear a closer resemblance to personal flights of fancy, to opposition to principles and to individual performance rather than what the company is really looking for, a strong cohesion, a consistency between services and a working towards company goals. This means that a real strategy has been defined, that the main tools of management are working properly in the company (performance reviews, meetings to resolve problems, career management, mobility) and an openness to real delegation of responsibility is foreseeable within the culture of the company.

It is clearly necessary to prepare the framework and personnel of the company for change and create a working environment which is ready to adapt before throwing yourself and your colleagues headlong into the search for initiative. Finally, and perhaps above all, you must be willing to rely heavily on the notion of trust which, itself, depends on the credibility of the senior management, that is to say, on the accord between what is said and what is done.

It's better not to launch straight into such training projects if it's only going to be a case of rhetoric and hackneyed speeches; once the fuse is lit it could be difficult to put out. On the other hand if the intention to seek personal development through the development of initiative is a strategic objective, certain companies have already understood that this difficult course allows them to establish loyalty among colleagues (executives and workers) and to give them new and ambitious economic challenges.

STRUCTURE OF A TRAINING SEMINAR ON TAKING INITIATIVES

Analyze expectations and needs regarding initiative
Make a list of questions and attitudes concerning initiatives.
Understand the need for initiative for yourself and for others.
Understand the company's need for initiative.

Analyze the potential for initiative
Allow the participants to know where they stand regarding their ability to *take* initiatives and to encourage others to adopt them.

Communicate the principles: Action – Reaction (I want – I must)
Discovering the active principles of taking initiatives.
Putting people in a situation of 'forced non-initiative'.
Objective: to establish the feeling of inadequacy linked to the loss of a sense or ability in order to demonstrate the impact on our behaviour. To show that other senses or limbs participate to take over from those missing senses or limbs to compensate for their loss. To show that the faculty for initiative is infinite even in the most restricted circumstances. The exercises in the discovery of these principles contain a high dose of psychology and should only be practised by specialist contributors.
The procedure consists of reducing the possibility for initiative by providing situations which provoke reflection (to imagine yourself in a boarding school, a prison or solitary confinement), or simulating situations with a physical dimension at stake (paralysis, loss of a sense or limb).

Process and techniques for taking initiatives (methodology)
Identify, measure and evaluate initiatives.
Prompt the critical faculties to get people to take initiatives.

CASE STUDY (PART 1)

Interview with Jack Parsons, Head of Technical-Commercial Section, Boss of Larry Baldwin.

"When I arrived at my office this morning, I found Larry Baldwin, one of my commercial technicians, waiting for me, file in hand.

'Good morning Larry, did you want to see me?' I said in a welcoming enough tone but thinking at the same time that I didn't have very much time to spend on him.

'Er yes. It's about the Major case, I can't seem to get any response from them.'

'I see. So what do you suggest?'

'Er... To be honest I don't really know, I was hoping you might have some ideas. Perhaps you could place a direct call to Mr Major, the boss. Coming from you it would certainly carry more weight.'

'OK fine, leave me the file and the phone number, but I have an appointment first so I'll call him afterwards.'

I went into my office and closed the door thinking that I have to take care of everything around here and that there is just no way of getting any of my employees to take any initiative whatsoever. If I had to tell Larry what he should do, I could just as soon do it myself."

In Jack Parsons' place, what would you have done?

Why doesn't he manage to get his employees to take initiatives?

Create a progressive process to evaluate the capacities for reaction and critical thinking.

Create a climate favourable to the taking of initiatives (demanding and tolerant).
Analysis of the company structure concerning the taking of initiatives.
Set up routes to initiative (principles, methods, tools).
Envisage the training session in two periods (eg two sessions of two days' duration) so that there can be an interim session to put the learning into practice where the participants will be taking initiatives, then do an analysis of these initiatives in the second session.

Take responsibility for an initiative
It is not a case of deciding during the course to implement an initiative but to agree to tackle some of those which crop up during the interim session. These initiatives could be based on a desire which needs to be satisfied against the backdrop of the professional activity. Those involved should be capable of explaining the ins and outs of the question (eg the launching of a new activity) or responding to a restricted or unacceptable situation from which it seems necessary to break free.

Going back to the interim session, each participant should be able to give a summary of an initiative and do an analysis of it.
Note that an initiative is often linked to reaction, and the necessary steps may oppose what is already in existence. This may cause ripples or waves depending on the initiative in question but be prepared to deal with resistance at all levels.

The courage to say no and the risk of doing so
During a training session or when we want to encourage thinking by our employees or colleagues one of the most effective tools to use is Stanley Milgram's work on submission to Authority.

CASE STUDY (PART 2)

Interview with Larry Baldwin Commercial Technician in Jack Parsons' section.

"Last night I waited in my office until half past eight for a call from a department manager at Major's.

To tell the truth it's a fortnight now that he's been keeping me hanging about, postponing our appointments from one day to the next. I called him four times in one day. The first time I was told he was in a meeting, the second time that he was with a client, the third that he had an appointment and the fourth that he would call me back.

I decided enough was enough. I'd have to go and see my boss. My position is obviously not taken seriously and it was about time my boss did something for once.

And since he was just passing my office I took advantage of the situation.

'Jack'

'Good morning, Larry.'

'Can I speak to you a moment?'

'Eh, yes what is it?'

'It's about the Major case' I said it as if he was in the know, just to flatter him a little, but hoping at the same time that he might ask me something about the case. But as nothing was forthcoming, I continued: 'I've been trying to get an appointment with one of their department managers for two weeks now and no way can I get any response from him.'

'Yes and so what do you suggest?' Jack asked me.

'Perhaps you could call Mr Major, you know him, don't you?'

I thought that I could then take it up from there, but he asked me for the file saying he'd look after it himself. So much for delegation! So if you try to take initiatives the file is taken from you. That's the last time I'll ask him for any help."

In Larry Baldwin's place what would you have done?

~~~~~~

~~~~~~

Why doesn't he manage to take initiatives?

~~~~~~

~~~~~~

From this case study we are made aware of the necessity for free will and the individual capacity to refuse to be blinded by a relationship based on dependency or hierarchy, and to allow each person to say 'no' to the intolerable. It is also time to highlight the notion of initiative by reaction and to provoke everyone to reflect on it or even put it into practice.

It is clear, then, that training plays an important role in the taking of initiatives and that good communication is essential for success. The following themes could be integrated into a course programme on initiative:

PROBLEMS ARISING FROM A LACK OF INITIATIVES WITHIN THE COMPANY
FAMOUS INITIATIVES
A TALK GIVEN BY THE DIRECTOR GENERAL OR MANAGING DIRECTOR OF THE COMPANY.

Final Point
EVALUATE WHAT YOU KNOW

As with all educational or training tools, this work should help you to evaluate your own knowledge. To do this we suggest that you fill in page 95. Then compare it with the sheet you filled in at the beginning of the book. For each element it is possible that your position hasn't changed or on the other hand that it has altered significantly. The extent of the change may show how your perception of initiative has changed and how it has developed from what it represented to you before.

Beware! Do not think that all your problems are over now that you see them in a clearer light. Certain elements deserve more of our attention than others.

Understand, however, that what *is* important is the food for thought supplied by the change in your knowledge and attitude towards initiative between the introductory and closing charts in this book. This will be the true value of this on-the-spot assessment. But more than a theoretical understanding of initiative, the aim of this book is practical: to promote the daily and effective practice of taking initiatives.

Furthermore, make an appointment with yourself in nine months time – a proper period of gestation during which time you will have integrated this new know-how and adopted new points of reference – by noting down 'my initiatives'.

Make a note of the chosen date:
APPOINTMENT FOR REVIEWING 'MY INITIATIVES'...../...../.....

This will give you a reasonable interval, so you will be able to fill out a fresh copy of the chart so as to evaluate the evolution of your ability to take initiatives and get others to take them also. (Suggestion: do this exercise with a colleague; this will enable you to compare notes later on.)

Consider the following anecdote:

The history of initiative
The scene takes place in the great North American forests. Towards the end of autumn, a woodcutter is in the process of chopping wood. An Indian passes by and greets him politely.

The woodcutter, ordinarily a man of few words, thinking to himself that Indians have the power to foretell events, ventures to address the Indian to find out if he should chop a lot more wood for the coming winter.

'Tell me Indian, do you think this winter will be a cold one?'

And the Indian answers in a friendly way:

'This year, winter cold.' Then he continues on his way.

A few days later the same Indian passes by the same woodcutter who is chopping wood.

'Hello Indian, so is this winter really going to be cold?'

And the Indian's reply is even more amiable and also more confident.

'This year, winter very cold.'

And so the woodcutter goes back to work with greater vigour.

The following week, they meet once again and the woodcutter, by now tired and worried, asks the same question:

'Really very cold this winter?'

'Very very cold,' replies the Indian.

The woodcutter turns to lift his axe once more, but intrigued, turns back to the Indian and says:

'But how can you be so sure that this winter will be very cold?'

The Indian pauses a moment, looks straight at the woodcutter and says:

'Old Indian proverb say: When the white man chop wood, winter cold.'

The implacable logic of this prediction is there to remind us that initiative is often a reaction and all it does, as in this case, is respond to an outside stimulus.

REVIEW YOUR CAPACITY FOR TAKING INITIATIVES

As you have already done in the introductory section of this book, but without referring to the original version so it does not influence your responses, for each statement tick off on the rising scale from 0 - 100, (0 disagreement, 100 total agreement).

0   20   40   60   80   100

1. I willingly take the initiative
2. I prefer to ask others rather than be asked by them
3. When I take the initiative, I feel I'm taking a risk
4. I make sure that others perceive or know about my initiatives
5. My initiatives generally meet with approval from others
6. When I come across what I deem to be a good initiative on the part of an employee or colleague, I congratulate them
7. When I come across what I deem to be a bad initiative on the part of an employee or colleague, condemning it is not the correct response
8. I would like my colleagues to take more initiatives
9. I want to be able to take more initiatives
10. The system, organization or my boss prevents me taking more initiatives
11. Initiative implies results
12. Initiative is an action
13. A company needs initiative at all levels
14. The clearer the objectives the easier it is to take the initiative
15. The role of initiative is to provoke a change of direction
16. Taking the initiative is something that has to be learned
17. Competence is a secondary factor in taking the initiative
18. Lack of recognition is what kills initiative

Finally, take a few minutes to evaluate your sensitivity to initiative, using the following exercise:

IDEAS ABOUT INITIATIVE

Note for each target concerned, one or several ideas for initiative that you could use regarding:

YOUR EMPLOYEES/TEAM ....

YOUR BOSS ....

YOUR PARTNER ....

FRIENDS ....

YOUR COLLEAGUES ....

CLIENTS ....

YOUR CHILDREN ....

OTHERS ....

The leap from looking at initiative as an idea to actually implementing it will evidently remain your own choice, but, if you want to take this step take care that your initiatives are always constructive and appropriate to everyone's objectives and ambitions. If this is not the case, it is time to reassess. If this is the case, your chances of success are high!

ALSO AVAILABLE IN THE SELF-MANAGEMENT SERIES

Get More From Life, Gilbert Garibal, 1994
Improving Your Selling Know-How, Sophie de Menthon 1993
Prioritize Your Time, Daniel Ollivier, 1994
The Professional's Self-Assessment Kit, Michele Eckenschwiller, 1993
Your Job Search, P Gaudet, M Estier and E Riera, 1993